EXCOMMUNICATED

WARRIOR

NICK KOUMALATSOS

DEDICATION

Excommunicated Warrior is dedicated to my beautiful bride. Without her this book would not exist. To my wonderful daughters who are my drive to be the best human being that I can be. To every veteran, father, mother, son, daughter, brother, sister, and any other human being that has found themselves in a life altering decision. I have empathy for your situation and want you to know that this book was written for you.

CONTENTS

ACKNOWLEDGMENTS

To my mentor, guide, and leader Karl Monger. Thank you for taking a chance on me and having the faith that I  would do the work that needed to be done. You saw that I had potential when I had no idea what I was doing. If you not had invested in me this manuscript would not exist and I would not be where I am today.

To my friend and guide Kirk Weisler. Thank you for lighting a fire that can show me the way. Your guidance has made me a better father, husband, teacher, and guide. I'm eternally grateful for your friendship and guidance.

To Dr. Cagan Randall, Thank you for digging into my brain and giving me the alignment that it needed. I was in a very different place all those years ago. I contribute the success I have had all starting back after going through your care. It is not forgotten  and I will continue to pay it forward.

Preface

For the first time in history, America has been in sustained combat for over a decade in multiple theaters with an all-volunteer force. This means that thousands of men and women have seen combat more than just a couple of times. This is a unique challenge for these people as individuals and for society at large. On average 22 veterans commit suicide every day and Nick, too, entertained the idea of suicide after he left the Marine Corps.

The Excommunicated Warrior takes us through a journey of Nick Koumalatsos' transition out of the Marine Corps Special Operations as he attempts to reintegrate into civilian life. Through this journey he found seven different stages of transition: apprehension, excitement, the bad emotions, depression, reaching an absolute low point, making a decision to move forward, and finally making it to the top. In the final chapter, Nick then shares his three steps to happiness and the secrets to his personal success.

As a veteran, Nick has a special insight into the struggles and problems facing this nation's veterans. This book is for the veterans struggling to transition from life in the military to life on the outside.

Nick has worked diligently to assist these veterans in processing these obstacles and feelings and working through this transition in his non-profit The Raider Project. But as Nick worked with these men and women, he soon realized that EVERYONE goes through some sort of transition in their life and that what he had learned could help not just his brothers in arms, but that it could help ANYONE who is going through their own transition.

In reality, every single human being will go through a life-changing transition. It could be losing a job of 20 years, a divorce, being injured, or retiring from the military. These life-changing events can sometimes develop into deep depressions and issues in every aspect of life. Some people never recover. When Nick left a 12-year career as a Marine Raider with the Marine Special Operations, he struggled to transition from one stage in life to another. Eventually, though, he took the skills he had learned as a Raider and got to work on solving the problem. This book explains the

process and lets us reap the benefits of his discoveries and

insights.

BEING EXCOMMUNICATED

I clearly remember September 16th 2012. The air was crisp and cool on that day. The sun was shining and there was a cool breeze. It was not so nippy that I felt chilly or uncomfortable. Rather, the cool air felt refreshing and it felt like a reminder of the change that was about to come into my life. It looked to be a perfect day. It had to be a perfect day because that day was the day I had been waiting for with both apprehension and excitement. September 16th 2012 was the day that I received my DD214, my official separation papers, from the Marine Corps Special Operations Command, Camp Lejeune, NC.

On that day, I had just recently returned from a trip to Greece with my sister and my father visiting family. This was my big vacation before coming back and getting my discharge paperwork and closing the chapter of being a

Special Operations Marine Raider. I had acquired about 120 days of leave that I had not been able to use due to the amount of training and operations that my unit carried out. Most Special Operators know that your leave and time off rarely fit into the operational schedule of the Marine Corps. We get a couple of weeks here and there, but for the most part, it is "go, go, go" and you end up losing at the end of the year. Luckily for me, it had worked out so that I could cash in my last couple of months with a big trip to Greece. I took off in the summer and I just had to come back to get my paperwork done. It was the ideal way to end one chapter and start anew. I had high expectations for the next chapter. In my mind, my new life in the civilian world was supposed to be exciting, happy, stress-free, and full of possibilities. Boy, was I wrong! Sitting in my car on that perfect fall day, I had no idea that my life was about to take a turn for the worse.

My trip to Greece had given me the opportunity to get a beard started. This was the classic first taste of freedom for most service members. My beard had not been as long as it was since my last deployment. I only had maybe a few weeks of beard growth left to restore it to its former glory. Nonetheless, it was not thick enough to block the cool breeze from blowing on my chin when I got out of my car. I had just pulled up to the main headquarters building of the Marine Special Operations Command (aka The Death Star, as it is known by people in the unit). It is quite ominous if you have not seen it or been there before. First, you have to be able to get on base, which for obvious reasons is not open to the public. Then, you have to pass through your second set of security to just get on the MARSOC compound. Once there, a posted security guard stands and monitors access control for every building. Again, for obvious security reasons. To outsiders, this was an intimidating place, but to me it was everyday life. I was an insider and this place, the base, the heavy security, all felt familiar to me.

So there I was, standing in front of the Death Star, gazing at the huge, brick building with reflective bulletproof glass for windows and doors. The door handles were made out of K-Bar knives, which are a staple in the Marine Corps culture, and in front of the massive building stood the flagpole surrounded by a memorial for every Marine Raider and Support personnel that we had lost. I remember reflecting on how fortunate I felt to be standing there, alive and well, about to get my paperwork and enter life as a normal person in the civilian world. I thought about how some of my friends were never going to get that chance. Instead, they would be right here, immortalized forever in this monument. I felt grateful.

I ceremoniously walked into the building and went to the administrative department to go turn in my badges and receive my paperwork. Honestly, I expected to be given the runaround for things not being done correctly. That was always how important paperwork was received in the Marine Corps. But this time was different and they just accepted my paperwork without any complaints or questions. I realized at that point that I was an afterthought. Twelve years of service and this was it. I had separated myself from the mission of the Marine Raiders and in return, they no longer really cared about my paperwork or me for that matter. They simply took my badges and gave me my paperwork. Hardly a word was exchanged and I did not even see or speak to anyone I knew. I took my folder and walked out the door. It felt like my life had just changed forever, but it could not have been more anticlimactic.

This was a foreshadowing - the first little glimpse of how I would begin to feel and I did not really fully understand it yet. I walked out the door and I heard it slam behind me. So there I was, standing next to the MARSOC Memorial in front of the Death Star, with the American flag flapping in the wind. I could not walk back into my unit's building, even if I wanted to. I was officially out!

While knowing that I had officially separated from the military gave me a feeling of excitement, it also gave me the feeling of eeriness. You see, this was all I had done in my entire adult life. My life had revolved around being a Marine and the binding set of shared attitudes, values, and goals that characterize our organization. It was, no, 'IS' who I am. The way I think, move, and communicate. Everything that I identified with revolved around the world behind the doors that I had just walked through for the last time. Nonetheless, I gathered my emotions and carried on, walking to the parking lot with almost a skip in my step, thinking, "I have made it... I am out, free, my own man, able to make my own choices."

I know it sounds silly to be so excited about getting out of the military, but you must understand exactly how the military works in order to fully appreciate the feeling. Even in Special Operations much of your schedule and life is dictated by the military. Now, don't get me wrong, the grass is much greener on the Special Operations side of the fence compared to being in a conventional force. However, as a former Special Missions Unit Sergeant Major told me, "You can be in the highest Tier 1 unit and at the end of the day, you are still in the Uniformed Armed Services and a SSgt in the Marine Corps." That means that you can't just call in sick. You can't just go home early. You can't use your saved up leave whenever you want to. You won't get a raise for being great at your job. And you are sure to miss big family moments because of long deployments. It's a great, but hard life with a lot of sacrifices and little freedom.

I got in my car and immediately took a picture (selfie) of my DD214 with a stupid shit-eating grin on my face and sent it to my team's group text message. Most of the teams I know have these and they are most definitely not safe for work, or children for that matter. My other teammates were happy for me, of course, and said nice things and sent inappropriate memes in  celebration of my well-deserved freedom. I thought this celebration was going to continue into the evening, but I was definitely wrong about that.

I'm not sure when that perfect day started to go off course. Maybe it was when I handed in my papers and fireworks didn't go off in celebration. Maybe it was when that door to the Death Star slammed shut behind me and I realized I couldn't get back inside. Or maybe it was just the lack of ceremony overall on this important day. However, things went completely off track that night when I immediately got into a fight with my wife. Honestly, I don't even remember what it was about and it really does not matter. What mattered was that my perfect day had turned into me sitting alone in my living room without my wife and daughters. There was no celebration and the excitement that I had felt earlier that day was pretty much completely gone. I felt overwhelmed. I felt alone. And I felt lost.

In many ways, I wasn't alone though. In reality, there are many individuals that are and will be in the same boat as I was in. You expect that there is some grand finale or some sort of acknowledgment of the huge achievement that is 'closing the door' on a career or a degree or whatever you've just finished. But there is not. There is no grand finale, like crossing a finishing line of a great race with everyone cheering your name. Instead there is just frustration, confusion, anger, bitterness, and worry. Now, these feelings don't come over you like a wave all at once. They often sneak up on you one at a time like being infected with a disease.

What makes people react this way? Why can't we keep being excited with the opportunities of closing one chapter and opening a new one? Personally, I had been a Marine for my entire adult life. No matter how great the new chapter might be, I was faced with the challenges that come with leaving something that you know. You lose the safety and the routine that comes with something you have been doing for years. This is the case for everybody, not just someone leaving the military – from leaving your wife to graduating college. You might have been unhappy. You might know that the decision is right for you. But that doesn't mean that the "grand finale" is any less difficult when that day finally comes.

So what exactly was I leaving and why? People would often question my decision to get out of the Marine Corps after so many years in. They would say: "Why on earth would you get out at 12 years!?" The implication was that I "only" had 8 years left before I would be able to retire with a government pension. Despite questions like this, many of the men and women in the Special Operations community choose to make the same decision as me. They also leave the military community in favor of the freedom of civilian life.

In 2012 when I left the Marine Corps, I had been a Marine for 12 years. I joined the Marine Corps in 2000. It had taken me just over two years to get the Marine Corps to accept my enlistment package. After two years of getting waivers for legal issues, drug issues, and school issues, I finally got my shot on the infamous yellow footprints. This is where Murphy's Law kicked me right in the pants. On training day 7, I broke my wrist. My recruiters could not believe it and I was dropped to MRP (Medical Rehabilitation Platoon). This is where recruits are held to heal until they can return to training. I worked hard and recovered in just two and half months.

I returned to training and quickly became the guide for my new platoon and ended up graduating Company Honor Graduate. That means that out of six platoons I was their number one recruit. It was a proud moment for me. After two years of working to get in and being injured during the first week of training, it seemed quite poetic to me that I managed to graduate as the Company Honor Grad. After a brief stint in the conventional Marine Corps and a deployment to Turkey in support of Operation Northern Watch, I took the screening for 2D Force Reconnaissance Company. Just being screened for the reconnaissance company felt like a dream come true. I was screening for one of the top units in the Marine Corps. I was even more excited when I was selected for training. I'd made it. I'd gotten my shot at something truly great.

I went through RIP (Recon Indoctrination Platoon) which to date is probably the hardest course I've ever been through. The purpose of RIP is for you to learn and get prepared for Amphibious Reconnaissance School (ARS) or Basic Reconnaissance Course (BRC). A little side note: ARS was closed down in 2008 and BRC is now the main schoolhouse for

creating Reconnaissance Marines. Anyway, I finished RIP and continued on with ARS and graduated. All of this seemed like the ultimate fulfillment. It was what I'd desired and hoped for. I was finally in a unit where I was treated like a man and expected to conduct myself as a professional. The standard was very high and everyone around me was on the same level as me, if not better. Prior to that point, I had felt that I was holding myself to a higher standard as a Marine than a lot of my peers. But as a Recon Marine, I now felt like I was finally like everyone else. This pushed me to constantly work on improving myself and ultimately become better than I'd ever imagined.

I had an amazing career as a Reconnaissance Marine. I went from being a Sergeant Slack Man (low man on the team), to Assistant Team Leader (ATL), to having my own team as a Team Leader on a deployment during Operation Iraqi Freedom. I had finally been promoted to Platoon

Sergeant and was able to influence new, young Recon Marines. At that time, 2D Force Recon Company had changed over to 2D Marine Special Operations Bn. The newly formed Marine Special Operations Command had integrated 1st and 2D Force into 1st and 2nd Marine Special Operations Battalions (which are now called 1st and 2nd Raider Battalions). I got my shot and took the Assessment and Selection to be a part of MARSOC and got selected. I felt fortunate because many of my Reconnaissance brothers did not. So there I was,

constantly proving myself and striving to be better. I spent the next five years at 2nd Raider Bn starting out as an Element Leader on a Marine Special Operations Team and finished my career with them as an Operations Chief on my team, conducting intelligence and operation fusion

Now, you may ask, "Nick, why the history lesson?" Because for you to understand my transition from being a Marine Raider to a civilian, you need to understand a little bit about the community I came from and how hard one had to strive and work to get there. It is the tightest community imaginable. Much like a sports team, it has to work together closely, but because of the frequent encounters with real danger and death, it is elevated to a completely different level than any other community. Not only do these men have to work together seamlessly, but they have to be able to rely on each other for support in combat and in life and death situations. On top of that we also typically relied on each other back in the States where we usually lived in the same neighborhood, our wives were all friends, and our kids all went to the same school. So needless to say, it was and is a very small and tight-knit community. In my opinion, I was a part of the greatest tribe this nation had to offer. I was never alone, I never had to deal with any problem on my own, or fight any negative force alone. I always had an entire team of 200+ bearded savages that had my back through thick and thin.

But let's return to September 16th 2012. I was out and on my own for the first time in over a decade – separated from the demands of the Raiders, but also separated from the community. I was honestly excited to be out. Yet, things slowly started to unravel and fall apart.

I had no idea why. I had been a part of the greatest team/unit/tribe there was, but now I was on my own with no support structure. My family did not understand me and didn't get my jokes like my teammates had. I found myself slowly feeling lost and detached. My tribe progressively stopped calling and texting. One thing that people don't tell you is that the Marine Corps keeps chugging along and the

Marines you call your brothers keep chugging along with it. Of course, this wasn't done out of malicious intent.

It is just that many of them continued on with their careers and their next deployment. They were busy. When you are on a team that is 100% your focus 100% of the time, then if you are not 'on a team' or 'on the next deployment,' then you are out-of-sight and out-of-mind. I had this belief that I would always be connected with my teammates whether I was on a team or not. But, the fact is when you leave... you are not connected to that community anymore and that is why it is so important to find a new one.

Over the next few months, I slowly started to slip off into what I call the 'Bowl of Bad Emotions'. From the outside, I had everything going for me. I had a job making really good money. I was able to continue to provide for my family, feed them, house them, and provide them health insurance. I had a nice house with a pool, a nice car, and a bank account full of money. Sounds good, right? Yet, I was completely miserable and lost. I had slowly started to gain weight even though I was still training. My health started to fail as well. I was not even sure what was going on, other than I was having issues with weight, my speech, and my sleep. I started to become extremely depressed as well. I kept asking myself how a man that seemed to have it all could be so depressed?

Imagine my 12-year career in the Marine Corps as a moving cargo train. For each operation, each deployment, each time you get injured, and each time you lose a friend and a brother, you collect another train car. It doesn't take long

to have quite a long train. And to add to this, imagine that while you are actively serving in the Special Operations you are constantly moving 300 mph. And of course the extra train cars that you are pulling are also going 300mph. Here is the kicker: when you leave the service or transition from any job where you collected some train cars going that speed and with that momentum, it's dangerous because when you go from 300 mph to about 10mph or even a screeching halt, there is multiple cars that will catastrophically crash into you in the most violent way possible. That is what was happening to me. My new life was not a 300-mph life. And I was dealing with the massive train crash all on my own. I was alone, isolated, with no support, and with no one who understood me. I was lonely, in pain, and I just had 12 years of baggage dumped all over me at once. Soon, I found myself going through a divorce, losing my kids, losing the high paying job, my health was failing, and I felt like my whole entire adult life was nothing more than an empty sacrifice. I felt like I had been lied to and I had just wasted my youth for a cause and a community that was no longer there for me.

This book is my personal story of leaving the Marine Corps Special Operations, of hitting rock bottom, of contemplating suicide, and of working my way back to life through hard work and dedication. At the same time, it is also a manual for how to transition from one life situation to another. I've outlined the 7 stages of transition that I personally went through. In my work with veterans, I have found that most people have to work their way through these 7 stages when making big life changes. My brothers and sisters in the uniformed services might find this book particularly helpful. And if you're not in the military, this book is still relevant since we all find ourselves in life-altering transitions at one point or another.

The book guides you through the 7 stages of transition, whether out of the military into the civilian world or something else. These 7 stages can feel like a rollercoaster at times. You are excited to be on your own and be independent, but that excitement is short lived. All of the sudden, you find yourself sad and depressed, and don't understand why. You are out of that old situation that you didn't want to be in anymore, you got a new situation going on, maybe a new job or a new relationship, or for veterans, a new life, and technically everything is okay, but you still feel like shit is fucked up. As a veteran you find yourself asking: "Why can't I be happy? Why do my spouse and kids suck? I just want to go back to the team and shoot bad people in the face again!" Every vet that I talk to goes through this same rollercoaster of feelings. It is unreal how we all deal with the same problems and ups and downs. I can take almost anybody's story and simply change his or her name and it will fit. There is obviously something to that. This book deals with the sad and depressing stuff that goes on behind the scenes in many people's lives as they transition from one situation to another in life. It's not a practical guide to finding a new job - organizations like the VA hand those out to veterans. This book is about the human infrastructure that we all, especially the nation's veterans, need. It deals with you and how you can make yourself physically, mentally, and spiritually well through these stages. How to make it to the other side and finally live a successful and happy life.

As I'm writing this, I consider myself a blessed and lucky man who in the midst of this personal disaster found some very positive people that gave me an opportunity to not only help myself but others around me. If it was not for this opportunity I could have very easily been another number in the suicide statistics for veterans. My heart is still heavy from the weight of the brothers that I have lost over the last 14 years. To date, the United States has lost 6,775 in both Operation Iraqi Freedom (OIF) and Operation Enduring Freedom (OEF), which I participated in. Along with the 2.996 lives lost on September 11 2001, that's 9,751

Americans who died because of the events of one day, not to include the 22 veterans a day that are committing suicide. We now have an entire generation that answered the call and took the fight to our enemies. That war has come with a price: an abundance of broken bodies, broken families, depression, loneliness, survivor's guilt, anger, and sleepless nights. I hope that this book can help some of these men and women through their transition.

I see people all the time pushing to be "successful" without really defining what that success means. Sometimes I think we can get so wrapped up in our personal vision for success that we might just miss it. Most people equate success with their finances: work hard, make more money, money pays for a better life, right? But what happens when you've worked your whole life and you're now "successful", but in reality you've neglected all your meaningful relationships and you've stressed so much over the years that you have health issues or can't sleep at night, and now you're rich, but ultimately also alone, estranged from your family and kids, and without a significant other? For me personally, every day I get new opportunities and see growth, I feel happy and thankful. Are these opportunities always where I want them? Of course not.

But, they never will be because I will always push myself to grow and be better and go outside my comfort zone. For me, success is about moving forward and seeking balance and freedom. Money is not my measurement of success, but a means to a happy and free life. Have I always felt this way? No! I had to change my perception of what my definition of success is. I worked hard each day to do just that and develop a more fulfilling set of visions for myself; visions that center around people, family, and helping others. I have made changes to my daily routine to support these visions. I had to see me myself differently and to push myself out of my comfort zones. Improvising, adapting, and overcoming each day. I can honestly say that working through the 7 stages of transition and taking responsibility for your own health and happiness is worth it in the end. I can guarantee you that even if you find yourself struggling or on the verge of giving up, that there is hope if you decide right now to never quit, never surrender and always move forward.

STAGE 1: APPREHENSION

I went through the first stage of transition before I had even left the military. This stage can strike you before you have even made the decision. Just thinking about quitting, getting divorced, or dropping your orders can bring on the first stage: apprehension. You will find yourself doubting whether it's the right decision to make. You might be losing sleep over the decision and you will overall have a sense of leaping into a big dark abyss and not knowing if you'll make it. To some people, choosing to transition from your current situation will feel overwhelming and frightening. You might find yourself quoting Ned Stark from Game of Thrones, telling yourself daily that winter is coming. And you don't feel ready.

It is scary to leave what you know and head for the unknown. It feels like a leap of faith. The saying "better the devil you know than the devil you don't" seems particularly fitting here. Coming from the military, the devil that you know consumes your entire life. I don't want to come off the wrong way when I describe how the military system works because it might seem like I am in some way criticizing the system in place. I am definitely not criticizing, but in order to fully understand this feeling of apprehension, you need to understand the lifestyle and system that is in place for every service member; a system that you will eventually become accustomed to as a Marine.

The first part of the military lifestyle that you get used to is the housing situation. If you have a family that is stationed where you are serving, then you are allotted a Basic Allowance for Housing (BAH). Essentially, it is a set amount of money based on your geographical area that is supposed to cover your housing expenses. This is an amount of money that you receive on top of your paycheck. And of course, if you don't have a family, housing will be provided for you on base usually. On top of this, you also receive a monetary amount for food. Your medical and dental is provided free of charge by the Navy Medical Corps and your family can also use this service for free on base or choose to pay a very small amount of money to be seen off base. You are given a very good life insurance policy in the event an injury or death. Also, the military command that the service member is attached to also provides support to families if they need it, especially during deployments. Essentially, the infrastructure for your life is very much established once you join the military. You don't have to lay awake at night worrying about being able to afford the medical bill for your sick kid. And you will always have money for housing. For me personally, you also need to keep in mind that I left home at 18 years old and joined the Marine Corps. So this infrastructure was all I'd known my entire adult life.

Throughout my time in the Marine Corps, I went through a good amount of deployments and the infrastructure of your life is planned out for you to an even larger degree when you are deployed or if you end up living on base in the barracks. You have a small room where you sleep. You only have a small storage space to put the few items that you own, most of which can fit in a large rucksack. For every meal, there is a place that you line up and get your tray and someone throws food on a plate for you. Whether you are deployed or back stateside living on base, you have a chow hall. I can honestly say that depending on where you are deployed, you might be getting some good chow. In fact, some of the best chow halls I've ever eaten at were in Iraq and Afghanistan. We are talking every type of cuisine you can imagine: Thai, Filipino, Mexican, American, Italian, and, of course, your normal military slop. Even when I was with MSOT 8222 up in Bala Murghab, Bagdhis Province, Afghanistan we had cooks that prepared our meals and a scheduled mealtime.

We would line up at the allotted time and get our chow, sit down at the benches with our crew or "gang" and commence to eat our chow until it was time to go back to work. There was a set routine and life was easy in that respect.

At the end of the day, you can lay your head on the pillow and know that your food is taken care of, your sleeping situation is taken care of, and your medical insurance is taken care of. Even your family is taken care of. Essentially, the military has your back all-around and many of the practical issues that you run into in civilian life are not even a concern for you as a member of the Armed Forces. This whole system reminds me a little bit of prison. When I was still in the Marine Corps, my friends and I would make jokes about old SgtMaj's being institutionalized and not being able to make it on the outside. We even called civilian life "the outside" much like a prisoner would do. Now don't get me wrong, I'm not saying if you serve you are basically a prisoner. We are very much free and are there by our own free will. I'm just making the analogy to highlight how much of an infrastructure there is in life as a service member. And when you spend your entire adult life within that infrastructure, you might just become a little accustomed to a life with such an infrastructure - you might even become a little institutionalized yourself without even realizing it. And like the prisoner, you might suddenly look at life on the outside with apprehension and uncertainty.

At some point, you will need to leave this system and this infrastructure. You will need to branch out on your own. Either you decided it was time or you were kindly told that your time had come and your military career was over. Now, with a few years under my belt I always say: "the end comes for us all." You can try and stay in as long as you want, but eventually you will leave the comfort of the military system and have to step out on your own like a brand new baby doe walking for the first time. This is not only true for life in the military. Nothing goes on forever.

The end of one stage and the beginning of a new is a transition that everybody has to go through multiple times throughout a lifetime. Whether it's the end of a life, a career, a bun in the oven, playing for the best professional sports team in the country, it doesn't matter. The end comes for us all and at the end of the day whether we prepare mentally, physically, and emotionally or not does not matter because winter is coming. What I'm trying to say is that all things, even your military career, come to an end. If you get pregnant, the baby will be born around 40 weeks later whether you're ready or not. If you have a career with a company, it will eventually end. If you are professional sports player, your career will eventually end and if you are a military service member, at some point the End of Active Service date (EAS date) will sneak right up on you. We do our best to prepare and manage the massive amount of anxiety that comes with this huge life change, but every life change is a huge undertaking. Embrace the journey and the change that comes along with it.

It was towards the end of my last work-up with Marine Special Operations Team 8222 that I started to play with the idea of leaving the Marine Corps behind. This was something I had never planned to do. But you see, things started to unfold in my life and I did not like the cards I was being dealt. Being the man I am, I did not like someone else dictating which cards I was being dealt in the game of life. My intention was always to stay in the service and get that sweet military retirement package. I say this with a sarcastic grin on my face, because while it is a decent system, don't be fooled to think you are going to do 20 years in the military and be set up for the rest of your life. No, you are going to have to get a dang job and keep on trucking, but now you are the old dude who is more than likely working for some young buck that doesn't know his ass from a hole in the wall... Good luck swallowing that pill.

As the work-up with MSOT 8222 continued, my conviction to leave the service only solidified for reasons we will get into later. We went on deployment and to date it was the best team and deployment I have ever been on. I feel very lucky that I ended my career as a Marine Raider with that team, serving where we did, doing what we were doing. However, during that deployment I had made the decision to get out. Now the work started to get everything set up for leaving the military.

Once you make that call, everyone looks at you like you just took the stupid pill for no reason. Why on earth would you get out at twelve years? Only EIGHT more and you are all set up with your cushy retirement. They were not 100% wrong and as you plan your exit strategy, all the worry and apprehension sets in. You look yourself in the mirror and realize that at 32 years of age you're going to take your wife, two daughters and stepson and you are going to venture out on your own for the very first time since the government started seeing you as a tax paying citizen. You realize that life on the outside means zero infrastructure, zero job, zero medical. Now it's on you, with no support structure and no tribe or team, to figure all this out. I'll never forget the time that a Two Star General laughed and said: "You want to get out in this economy! Ha! Good luck." This infuriated me! The audacity of this guy to think that I could not make it on the outside was unbelievable.

The truth is the unknown is what is the most frightening. I honestly did not know what I was going to do. I had a direction in which I wanted to go and I knew some people that might be helpful, but there were no sure things out there. In the military, I had everything, for the most part, taken care of for me or at least I was given the money to take care of it. Outside the military, I had to figure out how to get a job, get medical for my family, find a place to live, figure out what to do about the house we owned, and consider what to do about the kids' school. I was on the verge of getting out of the Marine Corps, my entire life was about to be turned upside down and it was all on me to make it work out! I'm a capable individual so I didn't understand why this was stressing me out. Once I'd dropped my orders, there was definitely no turning back. I was getting out! This was happening, I just had to figure it out, I told myself.

During this entire time of planning to get out, I knew I would have to deal with my physical issues at some point, too. I had hardly ever gone to medical during my entire time in service. I can tell you that there are some muscular-skeletal issues that you acquire along the way when you are a Special Operations Marine. So on top of figuring out my life as a civilian at 32 years old, I also had five surgeries in the span of 6 months between getting back from Afghanistan with MSOT 8222 and going on terminal leave and my trip to Greece. I'll never forget when the MD told me that I had the body of a 72-year old man. What he meant was that my knees, hips, back, spine, and shoulders showed significant wear and tear that would not normally be expected in a 32-year old male who was in the best shape of his life. The medical issues were in many ways fitting because on the outside I seemed 100% okay; I was blazing a trail to the future, even though I wasn't sure what the future was. However, on the inside, I had injuries and issues that hadn't even fully surfaced yet. I'll never forget how one of my best friends came to town and stopped by to catch up. He was a former teammate from 2D Raider Bn who I had been on a deployment to Afghanistan with. I remember telling him that I was totally transitioned and ready to be a civilian despite the fact that I had not even separated yet. He laughed and said okay, and added: "hey man, no rush, Rome was not built in a day." In my mind, I was already there: living a normal, happy, free life. But the truth is, I was only in the infant stages of accepting my new reality and the life changing transition that I was going to go through.

My entire adult life had let me up to this point. I had worked hard, pushed my body and mind to the limit. I had done things that most men would only ever dream about. My family and I had moved around so much, and been back and forth overseas, so I wanted to give my daughters a stable home. While I was in Iraq as a Recon Team

Leader, I identified the piece of land where I would build my house. This, of course, was in the Marsoc/Recon neighborhood. My daughters didn't really know what I did at the time, but just knew that daddy went away a lot. This was one of the things I was trying to repair. I wanted a stable environment and a solid foundation of infrastructure for them. All I had to do was figure this all out: figure out how to get a job that would pay me enough money to pay my mortgage and the rest of my bills.

But the more I looked I realized that the jobs I was qualified for were not local or anywhere close to where I had built my house. See, we had built a life in the area where I was stationed and I was not interested in leaving the life I had worked so hard to build for my family, nor did I want to spend hours commuting or being gone for long stretches of time. I had already had a job that took me away from my family and I was done with that. The area we lived in is truly great as long as you are serving in the military, but unfortunately there are not many high-paying jobs right there unless you happen to work on base and even then the money is not that great. So I found myself shouldering the burden of figuring out how to get a six-figure salary of any kind before my life and my bills would come crashing down on me. As a Special Operations Marine you receive more than just your base pay: I was receiving my base pay, basic allowance for housing, money for food, Special Duty Pay, Free Fall Pay, Combat Divers Pay, and, most months, Demolition Pay. And with the military, our medical and dental insurance was covered so that meant that for me to just keep what we had meant that I had to find a job with a six-figure salary. And that was just to keep our quality of life as it was. So as I was facing the end of my military career, I found myself shouldering this information alone with no community or support whatsoever. To say that I was feeling anxiety and apprehension is an understatement.

During this apprehension stage, you will feel the weight of the world on your shoulders. You will feel the heavy burden of having the responsibility to figure all of this out. Step one: get a new life set up – this might mean that you need to get a new job. But then it hits you: what if I can't manage to get a new job/find love again/get into grad school. Some people have a support system, but I had no savings and I had no family that could bail me out. Instead, I had a mortgage payment and I had car payments. I had groceries that needed to be bought and gas that needed to be purchased to go into the nice, expensive cars that I had acquired over the years with deployment money. You see, I had become accustomed to my infrastructure and our way of life. Now I had to figure out how to keep all that intact with zero support from Uncle Sam.

Just as the infrastructure of my entire life had been in place since I was 18 so had the community I was a part of. My community had only grown stronger over the years as I continued through the ranks of Force Recon. The Marine Raider communities were in my eyes a tight-knit tribe of people I could trust and count on. I had a perception that they would be there for me after my separation from the Marine Corps just as much as they had been in combat. However, once I'd gotten out, I found myself feeling alone and almost ostracized from the very community that I had always been able to lean on – the community that I so desperately needed at the time. I imagine that it can be compared to being an NFL player who gets hurt during a game and either is benched or dropped from the team. This young athlete at his prime has experienced an unfortunate incident that is derailing him from his desired path. On and off the field he has always had the support from his team, but after his injury, the harsh reality is that his team keeps playing without him, his team continues to practice without him, his team continues to win games without him, and his team will go on to celebrate those wins without him. The young injured athlete has become an afterthought and his fate, his direction, his success is now on him and him alone. He now shoulders the burden of finding out how to navigate this new world without his team. I was that athlete. On my own for the first time. I'd not only been separated from my career, but also from my tribe, and in many ways from the identity of being a Marine Raider – something profound had changed in my life and I was struggling with how to deal with it. It felt like I hadn't been ready to leave the Marine Corps after all.

Whether you are prepared for it or not, your life will never stay the same and you will have to face difficult transitions from one chapter to the next. Even if the transition is ultimately positive, it will most likely affect your life on so many levels that your identity needs to change along with it. The truth is the date, the time, the split-second that is going to alter your life forever is coming for you at some point. You can't will it away or plan your way out of it. I suggest doing your best to prepare, even if things might change (which they will). If you have a plan, then at least you can adjust from there and you won't be left feeling as lost as I did when I'd first left the Raiders behind.

The worry and apprehension stage is one that you just have to get through. You have made the decision or you are on the verge of making that big decision. Whether it is leaving the military, quitting your job, proposing to your girlfriend or moving to a new state, this stage will come to you. You can't let it affect your decisions because it is ultimately just a reaction to the fact that you are leaving something you know for something you don't know. You can probably make yourself feel more at ease by planning out some of the practical elements of your new life. And I urge you to think through some of the human infrastructure that you have to set up in your new life to thrive. You can use your apprehension as a check engine light that's telling you that you have things to do in order to ready yourself for the next stage. At the end of the day, though, you will just have to get through the unpleasantness of this stage. But I'll leave you with this: you might not have the crew, team, or community that you had before, but there is another one waiting for you.

STAGE 2: EXCITEMENT

FREEDOM – shout it from the rooftops in your best Braveheart voice! You have made it past the apprehension stage and you are now flooded by the thrilling high of excitement. You feel invincible and you are certain that nothing can go wrong. You don't think you will ever come down from this high because this is what the next chapter in your life will permanently feel like. You convince yourself that you will probably wake up feeling this excited every single day for the rest of your life because you have finally closed one chapter and opened a new. You think the transition was smooth and quick. You made it through the feelings of apprehension and now the relief of having made the decision washes over you. Personally, I was stoked when the day had finally come to pick up my DD214 - that precious piece of paper that said I was honorably discharged from the United States Marine Corps and allowed me to go about my business as a plain, ol', normal civilian in the great United States of America.

Unfortunately, I didn't realize that I still had a lot of stages to work through in order to actually feel like I had made it to the other side. The bad news is that the excitement stage is the shortest of all of them. You never want to come down from the high of this stage, but you will sooner than you think. And you might come crashing down and feel even worse than you did before.

The truth is, you have every reason to be excited. For the first time in probably years, you are free and you have so many opportunities. You are no longer bound by that rigid structure of the Marine Corps, or your failed marriage or your old job. It's exciting to feel your life move forward. We all find ourselves in this excitement stage at some point in our life as we make a big life change. Maybe you get a big job promotion. Or maybe you are finally retiring from a place you put 30 years of your life into. Maybe you are getting divorced or leaving a bad relationship and you are excited about removing the weight that you have carried for so many years. These are all valid reasons to be excited and you should very well be excited. This stage pushes you towards the future with a boost of positive energy.

I had chosen to extent the excitement stage with a big trip to visit family in Loutraki, Greece with my sister and father. For me, this was kind of my celebration trip for time well served. It was two weeks of breathing freely: no military, no kids, no wife, and no responsibilities. I could just be me. I could just breathe, smile, laugh, and the only person that was going to make fun of me or give me a hard time was my father. But that was a sign of affection and love more than anything and I knew that. I felt at home and that I was finally going to get to grow personally and finally figure out what it meant to be me outside the Marine Corps. I traveled all over Greece with my cousin and I can truly say that it was one of the most rewarding times of my life. I'm not sure if it was the company, the adventure, the timing of leaving the Marine Corps, or maybe a combination of all of it, but words cannot express how good that trip made me feel. It was as if I was washing off

12 years of dirt. To this day, I still reminisce about how each day of that vacation made me feel like a new person.

However, as all things, this trip also came to an end and I had to go home to pick up my separation papers, and move on with my life.

I still did not have a solid plan for what I would do with my life, but I was excited. My trip had left me feeling hopeful and refreshed. I felt as if all my problems would go away and I would live a carefree life as a civilian. I felt that all the things holding me back in my life as a Marine Raider were going to fall aside and never come back once I got my discharge paperwork. This was in some ways correct because I was really leaving a system that had been holding me back. The military has an inflexible structure for advancement, which means you can work hard and apply yourself and go faster, but at the end of the day there is a system and you just have to accept that and wait your time for advancements. Coming from this system, I truly believed that in the civilian world, success would be much more achievable. I thought that there was going to be nothing holding me back from getting promoted, making more money, climbing the corporate ladder, starting a business, or just being successful overall. While that is somewhat true, it's simply not that easy. You certainly have to put your fucking time in! Not to mention the amount of work, effort, blood, sweat, and tears it takes to make something happen for yourself. It is beautiful that we live in a country where, if one is willing to do that, success is a very real possibility. This idea made me excited to leave the military and start a new chapter on "the outside."

There were actually many things about my newfound freedom that made me excited: little things like waking up when I wanted to. Or not having to deal with meetings and work problems. I could let my beard grow, my hair grow, get a face tattoo, wear a pink tutu skirt and dance down the street if I wanted to. Not that I would want to do that, but all the restrictions of military life would be gone and I felt free. The possibilities were just endless and it was in my power to do what I wanted to! I felt as if the whole world was at my fingertips; as if anything in the world was possible. Again, while that is true, I had absolutely no idea what it took to make success happen on the outside. I had done very well for myself in the Marine Corps, in the Reconnaissance units, and in the Marine Raider communities, but, as I said, there is a structure to it. I wanted to get promoted faster than I was. I wanted more responsibility and I felt that the politics of the military was stifling my progress in life. On many levels, this was all true. You can meet the smartest person in the world, but if he is an E3 in the military, he is an E3 in the military and will basically be told to shut up and color. So for me, even as I continued to move up in billets (meaning what job I held on the team), my rank would only go up as fast as the big Marine Corps saw fit. This was frustrating because it constantly put me in a position of doing a shit ton of work and having a lot of responsibility, but not really reaping any of the benefits from this. Not to mention the fact that you are always treated according to what rank you hold and not according to the abilities you have. It is frustrating, to say the least. It seems like they need you and want you to do good work, but at the same time they don't have a problem never rewarding you according to the work you do. I was fed up with that system and I needed to leave. The next chapter sounded exciting to me.

So there I was in September 2012, walking out of the Death Star for the last time, DD214 in hand, excited to move forward, and completely oblivious to what was ahead. Ignorance is bliss and I was stoked! I remember driving off base feeling like this must be what convicts feel like when they drive away from the penitentiary - a feeling of freedom for the first time in years. The feeling of being your own man and not having your life's rules and schedules dictated by someone else. I was freaking stoked, thrilled, excited to be driving through those gates and seeing all of that in my rearview mirror. I had my paperwork in hand and I was a free man! Now everything was up to me and I thought I was SUPER capable so life was going to be easy.

The plan was that I would get my paperwork done, come home to the family and celebrate. I'm not sure if my wife at the time got Champagne or if I did, but that was the plan in order to celebrate a life well lived and an exciting new chapter! We had made it! We had made it through the entire marriage killing and dangerous career; through all the deployments, through all the hard times and this was the point of arrival. The grand finale! I was mistaken! I'm not sure what happened but my wife and I ended up in a huge argument that night. I'm honestly not sure if she started it or if I did something to provoke it, but at the end of the day it doesn't even matter. The point is that I always thought it was going to be this grand achievement followed by a celebration with my family, teammates, and loved ones. But it's not. There are no fireworks, you just fizzle out and fade away. I'm not even sure I heard from a single teammate that night. I remember sitting on my couch at the end of the night, having a drink alone and thinking "cheers to myself, for a job well done". The kids were in bed, wife was upset in the bedroom and I was sitting alone in my living room, drinking. No teammates celebrating with me, no family celebrating, not even my kids were around. It was just me alone with my thoughts. This is when it started to hit me what the fuck just happened. That 300mph train had come to an almost complete stop and I was about to get hit by every single train car in a major crash.

I'm not going to tell you not to enjoy the excitement stage. It has its value and it's certainly a major high to feel that rush of freedom and opportunity when you finally close a chapter in your life. I could probably have done more to prolong the excitement stage – organized a proper celebration that day for instance. But ultimately, this stage is short and sweet. Now, the excitement can come back once at a later stage, but unfortunately you can't cut line. We all have to go through the mud, experience the different stages of transition, and put in the work before we get there. The only thing I would really caution people to do is find someone to be there when the initial excitement stage is over because you might find yourself crashing harder than you ever imagined and in need of support. The next stage is when the ugly truth shows its face.

STAGE 3: THE BOWL OF BAD EMOTIONS

licated. Unlike the excitement

some people will never

s like every morning, you are

otions. These emotions are

difference, detachment, anger,

er, and bitterness. It is just as bad as

back at the night of September 16th 2012 when

had finally gotten my discharge papers, it is clear that things weren't as great and easy in the civilian world as I thought they would be. I found myself sitting alone in the living room with a glass of Knob Creek bourbon asking myself what the fuck had just happened with my life and how I had gotten there. I'm sure everybody going through a life transition can relate to this feeling of the excitement leaving you and the bad emotions starting to fill the void. It could be anything from the first night in your house or new place after a divorce or separation; the first night in the living room after burying a spouse, friend, or loved one; the day you found out your professional sports career was officially over; the day you were laid off from that job you put 29.9 years into and you just got laid off a month before retirement. Or, hell, that evening when you realize that you did everything right and your business still

times and you need to sign your bankruptcy p

During big life transitions like these, every single

ends up sitting in our house at the end of the night

drink in our hand, saying the exact same thing: "What

the actual fuck just happened!?" We feel alone and

overwhelmed. I think if we could get all those struggling

men and women together in one room with all of their

bottles and throw a freaking party to celebrate the

excitement and the fact that we have closed one chapter

and will be starting a new one soon, it would be so much

better for everybody. We need a tribe. Mankind is a social

species and we get messed up from being alone. Instead of

hiding in distress like a wounded animal, we need to come

together. Obviously, I know that we can't host big parties

for everybody all over the world that are sitting at home

distraught. But I think I would have benefitted from some

support and some celebration with my loved ones on that

particular night.

A lot of different elements played together during those

first few weeks and months right before and after officially

separating from the Marine Corps. My trip to Greece

seemed like a distant memory as I realized that I only had

another month and half to figure out a job and get my life in order or we would not have any money to pay for cars, mortgage, food, gas, etc. To say the excitement had worn off would be an understatement. It felt like a reality check. The outside was not at all as glamorous as I had thought. September is the end of the fiscal year for the government so contracting jobs were up in the air around the time I was applying for jobs. That meant that companies weren't really hiring because they were in the final negations of their contract with the federal government and did not even know if they would have jobs available. I was keeping tabs on all of the different companies that offered positions for what I was qualified to do. Now, with that said, I was not looking for jobs that required long deployments overseas. I had already done that and missed most of my daughters growing up. I know, I know, you can't eat your cake and have it too. But I wanted to have everything just the way I wanted it. I mean, I did my time, I served, and I gave, and I gave some more. It was my time to be happy and I deserved some good stuff coming my way. We will talk about entitlement in the coming chapters…

With each passing day, I grew more and more detached. I grew more and more dead inside. I had absolutely no idea what was happening to me. I mean, I didn't leave the house for probably a month and a half straight. I would check my emails and I corresponded with companies that were looking for someone like me. Because of the end of the fiscal year it was just a waiting game and honestly a lot of hoping it was going to work out. My last paycheck was coming on November 1st and that was going to be it. I definitely did not have anything in savings to bail us out if I did not get a check on the 15th of November. No rich uncle to take care of me if I hit hard times. It was 100% on me and while I was worried about that I also felt overcome by a ton of strange emotions that I had never felt before. I literally started to feel dead inside.

Remember all that baggage I told you I collected over the years? For the first time in my adult life I had stopped moving 300 mph. I went from moving that fast to the exhilarating speed of MAYBE 1 mph. My engine basically stopped! For the first time in my entire adult life I was hardly moving forward. And all the baggage came crashing down on me, inside of me, and all around me. I felt as if I was hit with a million-pound bag of bricks. All of the sudden, I was remembering things, especially relating to my friends and teammates getting hurt and killed in Iraq. I remembered the sights and sounds of the exact moments in which these things had happened. My mind was suddenly being bombarded with memories and thoughts that I had never experienced before and situations that I honestly didn't think I remembered.

Between the stresses of having to find a new job and the terrible memories coming back, I was not in a good place mentally. I lacked the human infrastructure to really see how big my problem was and it was hurting the people I loved and myself. I ended up swimming in that bowl of bad emotions every single day, all day long. Let's go through these emotions one by one and break them down. They will often coexist and mix in with each other, which makes it hard to really address them properly. You need to recognize the problems and feelings in order to work through them though.

APATHY:

I would say that being apathetic was the first feeling I really went through in all of this.

Definition of apathetic:

1: having or showing little or no feeling or emotion: SPIRITLESS

Example: She was listless, *apathetic*, calm with the calmness of a woman who knows she can suffer no further. - Frank Norris

2: having little or no interest or concern: INDIFFERENT

Example: *apathetic* voters

Every day I would sit on the couch with my laptop and answer emails for a few minutes once in a while. Then I would play whatever the latest and greatest iPhone game at the time was, which I think was Hay Day - a freaking children's game! I just felt completely dead inside. A mindless iPhone game was all I could mentally handle. Meanwhile, my wife wanted me to help with the kids, but I didn't. On some level, I couldn't. I was struggling with too much of my own stuff to be able to take on any sort of responsibility. On top of that, I did not really care about what was happening around me and in the lives of the people I loved. I was just focused on getting a job and getting through the day. Again, this only really meant a few emails a day. I wasn't truly trying to move forward. On some days, I filled out some random paperwork for a specific company that required something like that. But other than that I would just disappear into my little, stupid game. Now, when I say I would do this all day, I really mean all day! Hours and hours of just escaping from myself and my new life. I did not even like this couch life, but it was better than having to be present where I was and feeling what I was feeling.

INDIFFERENCE

Along with apathy came indifference. It was an emotion that I wasn't very familiar with beforehand. I was always someone who cared deeply.

Definition of indifference:

1: the quality, state, or fact of being indifferent

2a: lack of difference or distinction between two or more things

2b: absence of compulsion to or toward one thing or another

During this time, I became indifferent to everything. I was indifferent to everyone's feelings and desires. I just didn't care that my wife was upset for instance. I was indifferent to my physical fitness as well. I simply did not want to conduct any sort of physical fitness training. This was particularly worrisome because physical fitness was an absolute bedrock of who I was as a person. It had always been a fundamental and foundational part of my personality and suddenly I couldn't give two shits if I knocked out my workout that day. I did not care if I left the house. I did not care if my kids needed me or if my wife at the time needed me. She needed help and I just kind of shrugged my shoulders and did not even feel bad about it. What the hell was happening to me? This was not who I was as a person. This was not my personality. Something else was going on.

DETACHMENT

The apathy and the indifference made me feel detached from my life and my family. Since I didn't care, it was hard to really feel connected with the people around me.

Definition of detached:

1: exhibiting an aloof objectivity usually free from prejudice or self-interest

Example: a *detached* observer

The detachment took many forms. One of them was a physical detachment. I completely stopped touching my wife. I did not desire touching or any sort of sexual relationship. It had nothing to do with my abilities to perform, although some men actually experience a complete inability to perform in the bedroom during big life transitions, but for me it had more to do with the fact that I just did not desire any sort of sexual connection. Another part of this detachment was the relationship with my daughters. Essentially, I did not want to spend time with my daughters at all. I did not resent them and I wasn't angry with them. I just did not have the energy to act like I cared about what was going on with them or what they needed. This was out of character for me because I adore them.

It was around this time, unbeknownst to me, that my wife sat my kids down and explained to them what post-traumatic stress disorder was and that their dad was going through some stuff from his time in the military. She told them that they needed to be patient and loving with me as I worked through this. It broke my heart later on when I found out that they had had this conversation. Ironically, during this time in my life and prior to this I did not actually believe in post-traumatic stress disorder. I held the belief that all the men and women who were diagnosed with PTSD in reality were people with a weak constitution and they were just not cut out for the job. At this time, I did not even know what the symptoms of PTSD were. If I had been more in tune with that, I would have realized that I 100% had signs and symptoms of PTSD. During my time as a Raider, I just had never slowed down long enough to deal with the trauma or to recognize the symptoms I was showing.

LACK OF MOTIVATION

The lack of motivation was completely out of character for me too, but this feeling came around quickly as well. Definition of unmotivated:

1: not motivated: such as

a : lacking an appropriate or understandable motive

Example: *unmotivated* behavior

b : lacking drive or enthusiasm

Example: *unmotivated* students

I had spent a lot of time as a Marine being extremely frustrated with the people that only did the bare minimum and weren't motivated to move forward. And here I was, finding myself lacking motivation. I've always believed, and I still believe, that if you are going through life doing the bare minimum, that is what you're going to get in return. You're going to get the bare minimum return of life and that's not the way I ever lived my life and that's not the way that the people I surround myself with live their lives. The bare minimum is just that: minimal effort. I want to maximize my return on everything. I want to maximize my return on my career. I want to maximize the return on relationships. I want to maximize my return on physical fitness. What do I have to do to get the most out of everything? I am constantly asking myself questions like that. On many levels, I believe we have a systemic problem in this generation in that we're not applying ourselves and we're trying to figure out tricks and tips and whatever we can do to hack the system and get away with the bare minimum. To do the bare minimum - that is disgusting to me. Unfortunately, a lot of those people who only do the bare minimum are actually Marines. I was in the Marine Corps for 12 years and I saw those types of Marines. They are the bare minimum type of Marines. So if you're joining any job or joining any branch of service and that's your mentality, then that's what you're going to get. You want to be the most successful businessman or you want to be an Olympic skier? Guess what you're going to have to do? You're going to have to apply yourself and you're going to have to maximize every potential that your body and brain has. So it's all up to you and it's all about what you want out of your life. If you do the bare minimum, you're going to get the bare minimum. You deserve absolutely everything that you work for and you're entitled to nothing.

Now, that's how I'd always felt so to suddenly find myself completely unmotivated to do anything was hard. I didn't care about my physical fitness. I was unmotivated to train. I was unmotivated to live life overall. The lack of motivation was a doubly whammy in the sense that I needed the motivation to get better and to move forward, but it just wasn't there. The only thing I was motivated to do was sit on the couch with my dumb, little iPhone games.

ANGER

Somewhere along the way, I started getting angry. This started even before I'd officially separated from the Marine Corps.

Definition of anger:

1: a strong feeling of displeasure and usually of antagonism

Example: You could hear the *anger* in his voice.

Example: She found it hard to control her *anger.*

To say I was angry would be an understatement. I was actually extremely angry towards the end of my career. That anger shifted into rage after I got out of the military. I was angry at how myself for how hard I had tried at my job and gotten nothing in return. I was angry with all the shitty leaders I had had; I would work hard and bail these "leaders" out of trouble, do the work for them and they would still ever so lightly slide the dagger right in my back. How did they dare? I had devoted my whole adult life to this community and for what? Nothing, absolutely nothing, is what it felt like.

One of the stories that was running on repeat in my mind revolved around a particularly poor leader. Because of my background in Marine Reconnaissance I was taught to keep a solid patrol log on missions. I continued this practice into my Marine Raider days. So this particular

leader would basically sleep through a patrol or mission then once we were back at our Forward Operating Base (FOB), he asked me for my patrol log so he could fill out his own paperwork using my work and submit it to his superior without crediting me. This kind of behavior continued throughout this particular deployment until the end. Then this same individual had the nerve to rate me as the lowest of my particular rank on the team. For instance if there are five Staff Sergeants on a team, they have to rate them 1-5, 1 being the best and 5 being the worst. He rated me at 5... the guy that kept him on the team when the command wanted to boot him for his complete lack of success - the guy that had his back when he was sleeping on the job.

Another episode that I kept playing over and over in my head had to do with another "leader". I had this "leader" come to me when I was the Intelligence and Operations Chief for my Marine Special Operations Team and he continued to tell me that my leadership style was too soft; that I needed to be harder on the men and that I did not need to be friends with them. Nor did they need to like me. He went so far as to say: "You don't need to be their fun uncle", and so my nickname Uncle Nick was born and has not left to this day. Despite what this leader was saying, I was doing a good job and using a leadership style that the men responded well to; a style that made the men want to trust me. And then this Jack Clown wanted to throw some conventional, 17th century military hierarchy at me while I was running a Marine Special Operations Team comprised of just a handful of the best the Marine Corps has to offer. It was ridiculous and probably not that big of a deal. But in the middle of my anger, it seemed like a big deal and I could get myself worked up thinking about episodes and people like this. It wasn't healthy, but it was a way for me to process some of all the stuff I had been through that I had forgotten or shrugged off.

Needless to say I had clearly not gotten over incidents like these. My mind was an endless soap opera of every time I had gotten screwed over. It was like having my DVR stuck on repeat for the last 12 years of my life. I was remembering things from every deployment I had long forgotten. I was rethinking every decision I had ever made on patrol or in combat. Did I make the right call? And then I would get pissed off about the decision. Pissed off at myself, pissed off at the people I worked for. Pissed off at the enemy for putting me in that situation. Hell, I was pissed at America for putting me in that situation! I was furious because I felt I had gotten screwed over time and time again. This had eventually led me to getting out of the Marine Corps. I got angry when I thought about the fact that if I had worked for someone who was not a complete and utter piece of shit and who could have communicated better with me about what was going on, then I could have stayed a full twenty years and gotten my retirement. In all these scenarios, I was a victim of circumstance. I was a victim of who I worked for. If only they would have not been so insecure they could have seen the value I brought to the table. I told myself that the reason there was an issue was that I was too good and they were insecure in their leadership. Now, looking back in a more stable and rational state of mind, there is a lot of truth to that, but at the time,

I was using this to fuel my anger and to get myself stuck in the past.

BITTERNESS

The anger and the bitterness came together nicely as I was obsessing over my time as a Raider. I felt bitter because I wasn't in a good place, even after getting out, and all I wanted to do was assign blame.

Definition of bitter

1: distasteful or distressing to the mind : galling

Example: a *bitter* sense of shame

2: marked by intensity or severity:

a: accompanied by severe pain or suffering

Example: a *bitter* death

b: exhibiting intense animosity

Example: *bitter* enemies

c: harshly reproachful

Example: *bitter* complaints

d: marked by cynicism and rancor

Example: *bitter* contempt

Example: He was still *bitter* about not being chosen

e: intensely unpleasant especially in coldness or rawness

Example: a *bitter* wind

3: caused by or expressive of severe pain, grief, or regret

Example: *bitter* tears

    So check, Nick was angry. Then came the bitterness. I was so bitter I systematically started to surgically remove my Marine Corps tattoos. For you to fully understand how big of a deal this was you need to understand what these tattoos represent. On my left arm I had the coveted Eagle Globe and Anchor (EGA). The Marine Corps insignia, their logo, the banner that many a man laid down his life for. It was a symbol of laying down your life for your fellow Marines, your family, and your country! The EGA is on the Marine Corps flag, it is on the signs on base; it is literally everywhere and any Marine anywhere will tell you it means a lot! Actually, a lot is an understatement. It means an Epic Fuckton. Along with the EGA, I also had a USMC tattoo on my right forearm. I got it there so that when I shook people's hand they would see it right away. That was an idea I had taken from Marines of past generations. That tattoo came off in one fell swoop. Meanwhile, the EGA was removed in a three-part surgery. It was so large that they could not cut it out in one shot. They made an incision in my arm, took a section out and then sewed me up. Once that healed they would repeat the process, each time allowing the skin to stretch. The third time they took the remainder of the pieces out. There was a fourth surgery to take off the top and bottom tips which had become little rounded pieces of skin from it bunching up from each surgery. This whole ordeal reminded me of the movie Gladiator where Russell Crowe, playing General Maximus, is betrayed, his family killed and he is thought to be dead, but ends up in a Roman prison, forced to fight as a gladiator. There is a scene were the former General cuts out a Roman Empire army tattoo with a knife. This is what I felt like. I had become bitter and I felt like the very community that I had poured my

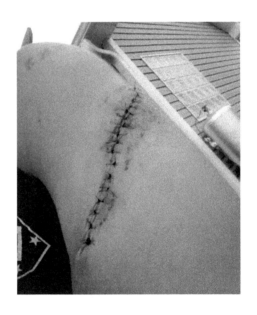

entire life and service into had betrayed me. So now I wanted nothing to do with them anymore.

I no longer trusted anyone that came from the community. I had turned away from my tribe. Friends that I had had for over a decade were not to be trusted according to my new worldview. I convinced myself that they only wanted to use me and that they were trying, in some way, to screw me over. I had gotten to the point where I thought that everyone was out to get me. There was not one person on this earth that had my best interest in mind, so no one could be trusted. This only fueled my bitterness and my belief that my whole life had been a lie. My service to my country, my sacrifice, my time away from my children, the lost teammates. All of it was for naught - just wasted energy. I had become a victim of circumstance and I was happy to stay that way. In the stories that ran on repeat in my mind I told myself that I had always done a good job at everything throughout my career and I was simply the victim in all of it. Everyone should have treated me with the respect that I deserved. The entitlement was oozing from me at this point.

There are a few things that I want to stress at this point. One: you are entitled to nothing! I mean absolutely nothing! You do, however, have a choice to work towards your goals and dreams. The fact is though, that even if you do work hard in life, you will get screwed over at some point. Guess what? It is not a matter of whether you will get screwed over or not, simply a matter of when it will happen. When it does, what are you going to do? Are you going to feel sorry for yourself? Poor you? I guess you could just wallow in that misery: "I should have been rewarded for my hard work", "I should have gotten that promotion", "I should have gotten that raise", or "My contract should have been renewed". Don't play into the victim mentality. This is life, we are going to get screwed over; that's a fact. But it is what we do after the fact that defines us and puts us on the path to our next great success. You have a choice: play the victim card and wallow in it, or shrug that shit off and move forward. Never quitting or surrendering your drive to be successful. Unfortunately, at this stage, I was not able to see this and I was stuck feeling entitled, bitter, angry, detached and indifferent.

So there I was in my new life, living a lie. I was certain that it had all been for nothing. No grand finale, no friends, no recognition for all the hard work put in over the years. Just all these negative feelings. I was apathetic to everybody's issues, but my own. I was indifferent to the needs of others around me. I was detached from the ones who loved me. I was angry at everything! I was bitter about my circumstances and what people had done to me. The Marine Corps had used me, the Marine Special Operations Command in particular had used me, and my leadership had failed me. They had used me because I was capable and then abused me to keep me in my place.

I was feeling 100% of these feelings all the time during this stage. The fact that I was feeling them means they were valid, at least to me. They might not have been reflecting reality, but they were my reality, which made them real enough to cause the issues that I was having at the time. If you have someone in this boat, you need to realize that their reality is just that - their reality. Their perception is their truth and whether or not it's the truth is irrelevant. This is where I often see families - wives, kids, parents – not understanding what is going on. For the person going through the bowl of bad emotions every single day, it's hard to explain. He or she has just started snowballing out of control emotionally. And it's hard for friends and family to watch. What you need to understand if you are going through this stage yourself is that your reality is valid and you need to deal with those emotions head on.

I had seen a psychologist once at this point. It was a guy that my teammates and I called the Wizard. His purpose was to assess your mental health and well-being. This assessment was supposed to be a fifteen- to thirty-minute meeting. Mine turned into a three-hour talk. The Wizard had just asked a few questions about my time in and, man, the anger and bitterness started to flow. I told him everything. Every time I had been screwed over, every time something bad had happened. I feel like I was making him sweat. It looked as if he had bit off more than he could chew. Did I mention I was angry and bitter? At the end of this I had worked myself up and I was even angrier. The Wizard, in the meantime, was wiping his face and taking deep breaths. At the end of the session he told me that I should probably go back to Greece and not make any serious life decisions for the next six months at a minimum. I laughed! "Yea right, man! I have responsibilities. I have a mortgage, car, kids, bills, and medical coverage. I can't just take off on a six-month spirit walk to "find myself". I'm a grown-ass man that needs to handle his shit." He kind of smiled and nodded, then gave me his personal card to reach out if I needed anything. I did not think much of it. For me, this was just normal. I didn't expect anybody to be able to understand me since I didn't really trust anybody. And I was used to the constant anger and bitterness flowing through my body at this point.

Around this time I had a couple of things going on physically as well. I had gone through the VA process screening. Upon exiting the service you go through a medical evaluation check through Veteran Affairs to assess the "damage" the Marine Corps has done to that machine you have been using to get you through your career. Now, the muscular skeletal stuff was not surprising: compressed lower lumbar, crooked c-spine, bad knees, torn shoulders - again, nothing that really surprised me. Having my body hurt continually to the point where I was chewing up 1600mg of Ibuprofen before a mission just to get through it was normal. The painkillers actually turned into a morning ritual. So being in physical pain, being angry, and being bitter was my new norm.

Also, during this time, unbeknownst to me, my testosterone had either started to drop or had been dropping for some time. This is pretty common in Special Operators and it is a trend across the entire Special

Operations Command. We have seen a trend of men in their early thirties with abnormally low testosterone levels. However, a regular doctor will tell you that you are within a normal range. I was told 200-800 ng/dl was the normal range for my age. I was at 240 ng/dl so I did fall within the normal range. Everything was fine. Yet I was not sleeping (I had not been sleeping through the night since 2009 and this was 2012, going into 2013), my energy was down, my physical strength was down, it took me longer to recover, I had a decline in libido (meaning I did not want to have sex), I had some new weight gain, my aches and pains were getting worse every day, and my mental aggressiveness had dropped. When you have low testosterone, you don't wake up wanting to kick the day in the dick. Instead you are just a sad sack of crap looking to figure out how to make it through that day with minimal effort. That did not in any way fit me or my personality normally. Those who know me now know that when my eyes open I wake up with the fire of Zeus in my eyes and the strength of Hercules ready to conquer all obstacles large and small, to kick that day right in the dick, to, let's be honest, continue to take over the world! So this sad dude that woke up and shuffled around the house was not me. I did not even recognize myself in the mirror. I felt as if I was living someone else's life. This could not be my life. This was supposed to be all gravy! I did my time, I put the work in, and I served my country - what in the fuck was going on with me?

So what do we do when we are feeling like this and not sleeping? Everyone knows, and everyone knows someone who does it: We start to self-medicate. If you are a veteran then you go to the VA to get your Global War On Terror Veteran Starter Pack.

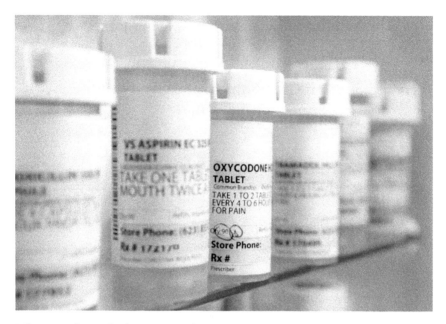

This pack includes something to put you to sleep, something to block out your dreams, something to wake you up, something to make you numb during the day, and something to make you focus on your work. I shit you not I got all of these in one sitting. They just opened a bag and said: "Here is what you take." Just treating one symptom on top of another and then taking some more for the symptoms you were getting from the medications. On top of that I was drinking heavily every night and, to be honest, most of the day. I did this to facilitate going to sleep. I justified it by saying that it would help me sleep better or just take the edge off. But every week I was just drinking a bit more and a bit more until it was a substantial amount each night. Little known fact: if you have been drinking, you will not get into Rapid Eye Movement (REM) when you sleep. If you take sleep aids, Ambien, Lunesta, or whatever else they are pushing, you will not get into REM. In case you don't know, REM is our restorative time in which our bodies recover and repair themselves. It is crucial to every part of our being. Our brain health, our memory, our muscular/skeletal system repair, our hormones, they all need to get into REM so we can reset and rebuild what we have broken down the day prior. Now, for me, I had not really gotten into a healthy REM cycle since somewhere around 2009 so I was rapidly circling the drain and washing it down with a bottle of Johnnie Walker.

STAGE 4: CIRCLING THE DRAIN

As I cycled through "The Bowl of Bad Emotions," I started struggling with depression. As I mentioned earlier, I felt as if I had been lied to: no brotherhood and no teammates to rely on, just alone with my thoughts.

Definition of depression:

1: an act of depressing or a state of being depressed: such as

(a) a state of feeling sad : dejection

Example: anger, anxiety, and *depression*

(b) a mood disorder marked especially by sadness, inactivity, difficulty in thinking and concentration, a significant increase or decrease in appetite and time spent sleeping, feelings of dejection and hopelessness, and sometimes suicidal tendencies

Example: bouts of *depression*

Example: suffering from clinical *depression*

Now, by this time I had gotten a job. Success, right? All my problems were supposed to be fixed now! That's what I thought at least. If I just had a mission, something to get me out of the house so I could focus on something other than myself, I thought I would be fine. This was October 26th. My end of active service date was November 1st 2012, right along with my very last paycheck. This job came at just the right time because they picked up my first check on November 15th when I would have seen a big goose egg! I felt like I dodged a bullet. And I essentially did.

I got a job working as a principal technical analyst, basically teaching Marines how to conduct Operations Intelligence Fusion, which is what I had been doing on my team before I left the Marine Special Operations Command. At the time this was a pretty important concept. The Operations world and the Intelligence world don't always see eye to eye or know how to effectively communicate with each other. That sounds like a bad line from the movie Office Space, I know. The Army Special Forces teams have had Operations Intelligence Fusion for a long time and we at Marine Special Operations command adapted it as well. When I got the job it was a good fit and I excelled quickly. At this point I threw myself into my work, just doing as much as I could and accepting as many extra assignments as I could. I was trying to distract myself from what was going on in my personal life with as much work as possible.

At this stage, I felt as if my tribe was gone and I was just fumbling through life alone. I did not feel connected to my family, not even my daughters. I can't remember having even one solid friend that I was connecting with on a daily basis either. I had work associates, but none felt like the brothers that I once had in the Marine Corps. I felt as if I had been fully excommunicated from a community that I loved and cherished so very much. A community that I fought very hard to get into and one that I had to fight very hard to stay within as well.

One of the reasons I threw myself into work was because my family life sucked. My kids sucked, my wife sucked, and I was just coasting through life like a zombie waiting to get back to work. My wife bitched at me because she thought I was working too much and not doing enough with her and the kids. I just could not escape the feeling that this was not my life. How did I get here? I felt as if I had magically been dropped into someone else's hell by mistake.

On the other side of this, I imagine my wife was thinking: "What happened to my life", "What happened to my husband". I'm sure my daughters just wanted a loving father to spend time with them and show them attention like I had done during my home time as an active duty Marine. Back then, when I was home, I made every minute with them count. This had definitely changed. When I came home I would attempt to train, although I had little motivation so it never really amounted to much. I would then immediately start drinking to wind down in an attempt to sleep. Looking back, I'm sure my wife was thinking she had gotten a raw deal. That she had put up with all the trainings and all the deployments just to get this shell of a person back at the end of all of it. It truly was not fair to her or the kids that this was the person they got after we had endured my military career. This was the time that we were supposed to be living life and be happy. However, all they got was a depressed, bitter, angry individual - a workaholic who could not be more distant of a father or husband.

I remember the night I almost broke. I was in my office at home late in the evening. I am honestly not sure if I was working or just piddling around to avoid contact with my family. I would often do this so that I did not have to engage and fake a happy smile or try to care about what was going on with them. I did not want to be touched or have to show affection to anyone. I did not want to be in some drivel conversation about their day. I just did not care. Remember, I felt as if my entire adult life had been a lie. Nothing mattered anymore. I just wanted to go back to my team. I wanted to go back to having a purpose. I missed being a Reconnaissance Marine; I missed being a Marine Raider. That was who I truly was! Now, after having lost those titles, what was I? Was this the life that I had to navigate for the rest of my life?! If so, then I didn't want it!

On that night, I was scrolling through some social media account, not sure if it was Facebook, or Instagram, or whatever was happening at that time. I remember seeing two of who I at the time considered my very best friends who were out to dinner together with their wives, having a good time. It was real and in real time. This wasn't even something I was imagining. And it was happening, as I was feeling depressed and having a full-blown identity crisis and craving the support of my former teammates. My mind was racing. There they were, casually going out and having a blast without me. How did they dare not to invite me, call me, or text me? It crushed me. It showed me that I was correct in my thinking about being alone. I felt that somehow I had made the wrong choices in life. Some step I had taken had been a mistake. How was I sitting alone in my office feeling this way and not out socializing and having fun with my teammates? Was this some kind of cruel joke? I remember cursing the universe for putting me in this position (see there… I was doing it again: that victim mentally). I was finished, done. I did not want to live this life anymore. I was so tired and exhausted of feeling like this in my head and body. I just wanted to rest. At that very moment I got up from my desk, grabbed my .38 revolver, ran downstairs, walked out the door, and got into my truck without saying a word to anyone. I was ready to sleep. Ready to be free from the pain.

I drove down to the beach where I loved to be. It was right around 9pm. Parked at the dock and started to walk to the south end of the island. I was so exhausted with all of these feelings. From not being able to sleep, from being angry, bitter, being numb, having the constant feeling of being betrayed, the feeling that everyone is out to get me. I just wanted to feel normal, but that wasn't going to happen.

This was my life and I either had to deal with it and try to survive or just end it right here. It would be over quickly, it would be painless, everything would just go dark and I would be able to rest for the first time in a long time. Hey, my kids would get their million-dollar life insurance policy. My wife would move on and find another person who she liked more than me. They would be set for life. I was the one in the way of keeping my family from having a good life. It would be best for them and everyone involved if I just ended it right here on the beach. They would be taken care of and I would finally get the sleep I so desperately needed. I started to scream as loud as I could, a deep roar as if I wanted to bring death to the world. I roared as long as my lungs could handle it. I roared until my voice and lungs gave out.

I remember starting to hear the waves crashing. You know that sound. They even put it in noise machines now to help people sleep. Something about that sound and the timing of the sets coming in just made me feel relaxed. The feeling of the cool breeze coming off the ocean, the sand beneath my feet going in between my toes. All of these sensations started to calm me. I was exhausted. While breathing heavy from the screaming the waves reminded me of my daughters and the times I would bring them down to the beach when I was home between deployments or training exercises. I started to see their faces running away from the waves as if they were being chased by funny monsters, only to turn around and chase them back. I took a big breath, put the .38 in my pocket and walked back up the beach to my truck. When I got home I remember the look on my wife's face. She just stood there and did not say a word, she was white as a ghost and did not say a word. I grabbed the whiskey, poured a glass and sat down on the couch.

Let's discuss this suicide thing. It's something I am all too familiar with both within our veteran community as well as the civilian community that I'm now a part of. I never wanted to be dead. I did not want to kill myself. I just wanted peace and rest. I was contemplating making a permanent solution to a temporary problem. I do not believe that veterans, or anyone for that matter, kill themselves because they actually do not want to live. I believe they do it because of the pain, the exhaustion of dealing with their problems so ultimately they are just looking for an escape. I believe that people that commit this horribly selfish act are actually just craving rest, not death.

We know now that the second and third order effects of a suicide on a family are astronomical. This is an event that will plague a family for generations if not dealt with appropriately. It is like a plague that can infect every one of the younger generations. If little Jimmy's father or mother commits suicide, then what is stopping from little Jimmy from committing suicide when things get tough later in his own life. Jimmy is going to say: "Well, mom or dad did it, so it's an option." We have now seen that where there is one suicide in the family, there tends to be another later on. As a father I would never want the idea of suicide to be a thought that my children would even entertain.

At this stage in my life, I was battling an identity crisis. Who the heck was I if not a Recon Marine or a Marine Raider? I was battling low testosterone, an undiagnosed traumatic brain injury, and I was completely in denial that post traumatic stress was a real thing, let alone the fact that I had any symptoms at all. All this led me to the beach on that night.

Before we move on, let's talk about social media. Social media can be an amazing tool. It has revolutionized my business and life. Hell! It is the reason that you are reading this book and the reason I got to write it in the first place. I met my current wife through social media. However, for the person who is battling what I was or a person who is not in a healthy place, it can be the worst possible thing in your life. We see it all too often; you end up comparing yourself and your happiness to that of others. You use it as a measurement of success in your life, constantly comparing your success to that of others. You compare your relationships and the happiness of your closest relationships to what you see on some Instagram post. I'll tell you right now, as someone who is in the media business: what you see in a picture or in a video is not always the truth. I've become quite the photographer and videographer. It is my job to make the subject I'm shooting or the story I'm trying to tell appear in the best way possible. I always try to make them look their very best, almost like something out of a hallmark card. But the dirty truth is that it simply is a lie. If you base your feelings on or if you compare yourself to those pictures on social media, then you are comparing your life to a bunch of lies.

Let's look at my two very good friends that were out having dinner with their wives and posted about it on social media. Do you think they intentionally left me out? Yes and no. You see, there is a paradigm shift when you get out. Once you get out, you start the clock on your transition. From the inside looking out, Nick had gotten out and was living life. He was with his family, being happy. He had a really high paying good job and had moved on from the team. So without knowing it they did the exact opposite of what I actually needed. They thought that I was good and needed to spend time with my family and that honestly, I really did not want to do the military thing anymore. Ironically, once they got out they went through very similar experiences and we connected with each other about this exact subject. It was an emotional and difficult conversation, but amends were made and we have worked together these past years to ensure this does not happen to more of our community or the circles we travel in.

Let the work begin.

STAGE 5: SINK OR SWIM

After getting close to committing suicide, I entered the next stage. I call it the sink-or-swim stage. This is where you decide whether you want to live and work on getting better or whether you want to call it quits.

This portion of the story is not a couple of months. This portion is more along the lines of almost two years. About a month after that incident on the beach I received my paperwork back from the VA. I was shocked! These idiots diagnosed me with Post Traumatic Stress Disorder. What the hell?! I did not have PTSD; that was for the weak! I'm a man! I could handle my job and what I did. How did they dare to label me with such a poisonous term?

Meanwhile I was actually exhibiting a lot of symptoms of PTSD. On an almost daily basis, I was having flashbacks to things that had happened six years ago in Iraq with my Reconnaissance Platoon. To say that that deployment was a rough one would be putting it lightly. It was during the surge of Operation Iraqi Freedom and we were serving in Fallujah. We suffered too many casualties; and I phrase it that way because even just one is too many. But here I was, a civilian, six years later in my house having dreams about those days and seeing some of my brothers that we lost in Iraq in my daily life. I could be driving down the road and I would see a group of Marines standing there, except my mind would play a trick on me and one of them would be a dead teammate, so I would turn around to go check if I had actually seen my fallen brother. I rationally thought that there was no way this man was alive, but I had to check. This happened multiple times as well as all the other stuff that was going on.

It had been a while since I had talked to all of my old Recon Marines because I had left that command and gone straight to 2D Marine Raider Bn. As I mentioned previously, my train continued moving 300 mph throughout my career so I never slowed down to process anything. But with the constant flashbacks and the PTSD diagnosis from the VA, I was finally forced to deal with everything.

I called one of my good friends, Tony Cano. I decided to tell him what had been going on with me and how I felt like I was losing my mind. I told him that I had been seeing Gary Johnston and Dustin Lee randomly throughout my day. He kind of chuckled at me, not in a bad way, but then proceeded to tell me: "Yea man, welcome to the club, almost everyone from that platoon has had issues for a long time." You see, most of that platoon had gotten out of the Marine Corps after that deployment so for the last six years they had been having to deal with all of that. I come to find out that there was a host of issues within that group of guys with substance abuse, legal issues, divorce, homelessness, and mental health. I mean, you name it and it had happened to our guys, and this included suicide. Tony told me that he also had been dealing with some issues and he was very glad that I called. He said that I was not alone in feeling that way and I was just catching up on what had happened. Around this same time I caught up with another good friend who laid out a great analogy for me. He said it was like having everything you experience in life being poured into a bucket of water. If you keep living and experiencing things that are filling that bucket up it is only a matter of time before that bucket will overflow. How does it overflow? It overflows into broken relationships, it overflows into substance abuse, and it overflows into financial issues, employment issues, and legal issues. If we don't deal with the water, we will have a mess on our hands.

As I was figuring all of this out and still struggling to find my footing, my wife at the time called it quits. Now, there are tons of reasons why. I can't fully blame it on my transition out of the military. I do believe that it sucked for both of us. I felt as if I was a different person and not the person she wanted or needed. Neither of us was really happy or had been giving each other what we needed because at the core, we wanted and needed different things. We had been separated four different times throughout the years for almost the same reasons. Keep in mind that out of 12 years of marriage, I had been gone six of those years. Of those six years we were never consecutively together for more than six months at a time. How can people grow together when they are not actually together? Essentially, we grew apart and were not the people that we once were. Whether it was the right call or not, divorce is extremely painful and when a veteran or anyone is going through this change of life or identity it can cause things that they are dealing with to escalate. At first, it felt as if a burden had been lifted with the end of my marriage, but the reality set in and the transition from having a family to the feeling of losing my daughters and the way things once were destroyed me on the inside.

Remember that good job I had? Well, I was still working there and had already gotten a promotion. I had been networking for almost a year and making things happen for myself in the professional arena. So, while my professional side was going well, it was my personal side that was gravely suffering. So in some ways, I looked successful. At this time, just about a year after I had gotten out, a lot of my old teammates and some other guys happened to be leaving the service and they started to show up on my doorstep asking for advice. They would be saying things like: "What should I do? How do I navigate the VA? What am I going to do about health care? What about a job? What is available?" They were in that stage 1 of worry and apprehension. So me being naïve I thought, if I could use the networking that I had done in the past year and get these dudes a job then everything would be A OK, just like they were for me. Except things weren't really OK for me. Hindsight is a bitch! Anyway, I started to put together trips to networking events to get these guys set up. We paid for it out of our own pocket with me orchestrating it. My thought was that if I could get guys in front of the program managers, Vice Presidents, Presidents, and Owners of companies and show them what these veterans brought to the table, then we could bypass the Human Resources office who did not have the first idea what a Marine Raider was or what they were capable of. I thought that all I had to do was get a guy a job and that would make them healthy, happy, and stable.

During one of these events I had met Karl Monger, the Executive Director of GallantFew. GallantFew is a non-profit organization whose sole mission is to assist in a successful transition of veterans into the private sector. He found out what we were doing and told me that what I was doing was veteran service organization work and that I should structure it and develop some infrastructure so that we could scale it and help more Marines. Through a few more conversations, that is exactly what we did and we created an organization under GallantFew called The Raider Project. Karl Monger would later go one to being one of my most important mentors through my transition and growth into what I like to call a "Full Human Being".

Before we move on to the nitty-gritty of things, I want to put some stuff in perspective: This generation of warfighters has made American history. Never before in our history have we been in sustained combat in multiple theaters (countries) for as long as we had been with an all-volunteer force. Even though I know the Vietnam War was long, and I certainly do not want to take away from those amazing heroes that had to endure that fight, it was not the same because up until 1973, when we pulled out of Vietnam, we were a draft service. I personally have a lot of positive thoughts regarding that. But when we talk about long conflict and the infrastructure of the military war machine, we have to take this into account. See, back then, the majority of these men were drafted and did one, sometimes two, very difficult and long deployments. However, in this conflict we have been 100% an all-volunteer force. With guys in the upwards of 5-8 deployments, some even more. Now I'm talking 5-8 actual combat deployments. On top of that, I want you to think about something: We have all seen the typical information about the 2nd and 3rd order effects of the men that came back from WWII, Korea, and Vietnam. If it is as bad as it was with a force that was drafted and where most only did one deployment, I ask you this… What will be the 2nd and 3rd order effects when it comes to this generation serving in the Global War on Terror in multiple theaters who has volunteered to go on 5-8 deployments in a combat zone? Before leaving the Marine Corps, I had been ignoring all of these issues, simply because I had never really had to deal with them. I had thought that life was going to be easy after the military.

What if someone tells you that six months after leaving the military, you would want to commit suicide? I don't think you would have believed them, but you would have been better off once you were going through the stages of bad emotions and depression. Now, if someone told you that things would be difficult even just a few months after quitting your job, getting a divorce, moving to a new area, or going through whatever life transition you were going through, then what would happen? If I told you that and you heard me clear as day and it was seared into your memory, what do you think happens when you get to that point? Does it take the power away from the depression and the suicidal thoughts? I believe it does. Because, instead of having these feelings and either not understanding them or being absorbed by them, you might just go: "Hey! Nick said that this was going to happen and this is what I needed to do about it." The old adage: "Knowledge is Power" is 100% correct here. It is empowering to know what is going on with your body and mind. Not understanding what is going on can make someone feel crazy. So I would rather be prepared and armed with the knowledge of the path I was about to take than wander through the dark aimlessly.

This is where we have a choice to either sink or swim. Do we get to advance in the game of life or do we lose? Only difference is that in this game there are no do-overs, no re-spawn, no go to jail and wait your turn for another round. It reminds me of being in Combatant Dive School in Panama City, Fl. One of the portions of training to become a Combatant Diver is something called Emergency Procedures (EP's) also known as HITS, which will make more sense in a minute. The diving exercise is conducted in a pool so that it is a safe and controlled environment, well monitored by the staff and by a medical crew as well. Before anyone goes all Mothers of America on me or the training, let me say it was some of the best training I've ever done right along with the captivity portion of Search, Evasion, Resistance, and Escape training (SERE). The objective of this dive training is essentially to learn to self-rescue or recover from a near-catastrophic incident under water. You could have been hit by a boat or caught in bad surf, either way one needs to know how to stay calm, cool, and collected because when or if it happens in real life, it's just you and your dive buddy down there and no grownups to save you.

Here is how the diving exercise goes: You have all your dive gear on, you are breathing comfortably with a big pair of silver twin 80's on. Twin 80's are two scuba tanks that have a cycle for a reserve in the event you need more air or have to stay under longer than expected. As a side note, every combatant diver is expected to have the ability to tread water for sixty seconds with their head above water with no inflatable device. So here I was, down at the bottom of the pool, just swimming along, minding my own business when a great wave of destruction came over me! My mask was ripped from my face making my vision blurred. My regulator (device that supplies air to me) was ripped from my mouth. I was getting thrown all over the pool, suddenly not sure which way was up or down anymore. I was completely disoriented and I was getting elbowed in the ribs, which caused me to lose some of my breath. And did I mention that this cluster fuck started to happen when I was mid-breath so I did not even have a full breath of air. When the wave of destruction had stopped, I realized that they had turned off my air and pressed the valve on the air to completely get rid of any air in the hose. This gave them the ability to wrap my hose around the tanks and regulator to make a huge mess of a knot. Then they proceeded to turn the air on in order to inflate the tube so that it tightened the knot even more. So I was disoriented and quickly running out of air. In this situation, I had a few options: I could quit the exercise by taking the safety diver's spare regulator and getting a quick breath of air or I could bolt to the surface of the pool, but that would be an immediate dismissal from the school for being a safety risk to myself. You see, if you bolt to the surface while breathing compressed air and you do not off gas, meaning blow all your air out as you ascend up towards the surface, you can essentially over-expand your lungs causing them to burst with oxygen getting into your bloodstream too fast which quickly goes to your head, making some really gnarly shit happen to you leading up to your death. So needless to say, that's a no go option.

In that situation, I chose to figure my shit out; stay cool, calm, and collected. My regulator was on, but it was right up against my tanks. I could not pull on it, but it was sticking out just enough to get my mouth on it and get a much-needed breath of air. I had taken my tanks and put them in front of me so that they could not be taken from me again. I continued to take slow steady breaths that slowed my breathing down and overall calmed me down. Once I had collected myself, I cycled my air off and bled the regulator of any remaining air. This loosened the hoses and allowed me to undo the knot with a little work. Once the knot was undone I put the regulator back in my mouth and cycled the air on. Then I just sat on the bottom of the pool fixing my straps and my gear situation. Once I squared myself away and gave the instructor and safety diver the "OK" symbol, they gave me my mask back and I continued on my way swimming around the bottom of the pool. Did I mention that the instructor that happened to cause this wave of destruction was coming from the top of the pool and did so on a breath hold - keeps things interesting and honest. What makes it even better is that this was just one of many rounds. We did this several times...

You might be asking yourself: "What the heck, Nick! What does that have to do with my life or this situation I'm in?" Well, I had a choice. I could quit and take the temporary fix by taking the guy's reserve hose to get some air. But then I would still be left with a shitty situation on my end. No matter how much of his air I use, my situation is still fucked and I'm just going to keep staring at it until I do something about it. Then the other option is to go straight up and make a hard QUIT and bail to the surface, possibly causing death or permanent damage to yourself. The way I see it is that using the safety hose is like drinking that bottle of Johnnie Walker or popping all of those lovely pills the Doc so freely gives out to mask the real situation.

But, no matter what we do with temporary fixes like that, the situation is still fucked. Bailing on your situation and bailing on your life - to me that is just clocking out and quitting, quitting on your teammates, your friends, and your family. To me my team, my friends, and my family are worth putting the work in for. Fortunately, there is a third option: to keep swimming, to not give up, to undo the knots, and get back to a place where you can sustain yourself again.

Let's get back to the problem at hand: I had an option to sink or swim in my life after the Marine Corps. As much as I wanted to rest I did not want to sink. I was not a quitter; I had never been a quitter. My whole life had been one test after the other of my perseverance through adversity. I had to figure out the problem with my gear. Unfortunately, that was going to cause a lot of pain and a long road.

My experience was not that different from that of anybody in this stage of his or her transition. You might be a person with a substance abuse issue after getting divorced. You cannot get help or really be helped until you admit you have an issue. Your hose has been detached and you've experienced the life equivalent of an underwater cluster fuck. You might not actually realize that you want the help in the first place. I had to get to a place that I actually wanted to be helped. Unlike the diving training, nobody had ever taught me exactly how to respond to a situation like the one I was in. I didn't know how to move on, but at least I had realized that I needed to get help and that I needed to take responsibility and fix the situation.

STAGE 6: PUTTING IN THE WORK

Who remembers Pac-Man? My better half, Miss Capra, gave me an analogy once that really stuck with me. Sometimes I feel like the little yellow guy just trying to get the cherry, but I have these ghosts trying to get me. The closer I get to the cherry, the faster the ghosts are coming at me. Just as I'm about to get the cherry, the ghosts get me, and I have to start over. The only way to get away from the ghosts and get the cherry is to keep juking and even go backwards or sideways to get the cherry. But, if you don't give up and don't quit, then once you get that cherry, what happens? It gives you power so that you can turn around, fuck them ghosts up and watch them all turn and run.

For me personally, this stage of putting in the work was a very long one. I feel like this stage has different levels or more correctly put, you feel as if you are riding a roller coaster of personal ups and downs. In anybody's life there are high points and low points. As we are working on ourselves, whether it is overcoming a traumatic situation, figuring out our identity after a career change, or overcoming a divorce, we are all going to have high points and low points. What we hope to happen is that those lows aren't so low and the highs aren't so high. We hope that we

Nick Koumalatsos

through this work can level out our life, becoming more emotionally and mentally stable people.

Now, by this time I had fully gone through my separation from my wife. My ex-wife had taken my two beautiful daughters and moved them to Tennessee with hopes of starting a new life. I felt guilty for ending things and for me not being who I once was so I thought it was best if she had a shot at a new life, leaving this one behind. This was something I would regret later.

Remember that awesome job I had? I was about to get a wakeup call and get sucked back into the real world. It was a Monday afternoon in my secured building. We had 26 Marines in my classroom going through a course I had designed. One of my co-workers and friends was assisting the Marines with their work and I was on a secured network assisting three Marines overseas in Afghanistan, supporting Operation Enduring Freedom. I got a call from the lead at my company, saying he needed to talk to me. I told him I was swamped with Marines and would have to call him back. He said okay, but hurry. When I had to take a break to pee I ran into the bathroom and called him while I was taking a leak. He answered and dropped the news on me mid-stream. My contract was terminated… right there

114

in the middle of the day with 26 Marines in my office and three overseas, waiting for my help. I came out of the bathroom, grabbed a small box to put a few of my things in and left. That was it and just like that I was unemployed. Later I would find out that the system my team and I had developed was going to be adapted by the main company and spread company-wide. Somehow, I did not seem to fit into their plan. Because I worked for them at the time anything I created was their intellectual property and I could not make any claims to the system or processes. The way this job had worked was that I was a subcontractor who worked for a company that had a contract with the main company. The main company was the one that canceled my contract, but the company I worked for directly was kind enough to keep me on for another 2.5 months to work on a project they had needed people to do and I happened to be the lead on the information that they needed for the project.

About three months before this, I had actually started my first company, Survival and Tactical Systems. I wasn't sure what that exactly was or what I was going to do with it. Initially I thought I would use it as a pass-through for my taxes to assist with writing off specific work-related equipment. At this time, I had also started the whole thing with The Raider Project with Karl Monger and the rest of the GallantFew. Needless to say, I had some things keeping me busy.

I was still working through my issues or, to be brutally honest, I had at least recognized that I had some issues. I can't say I was working on them because I was clueless in terms of how to do that. Nonetheless, I was doing my best to move forward. I was struggling to grow my business and even trying to figure out what that business was. I know, not a great plan for someone who was generally feeling kind of lost. I felt as if I was in a fog. There was no clear vision for either my business or the non-profit I was attempting to build. To make it worse I only had about fifteen thousand saved up that had to get me through to the next thing. I had actually gotten a job offer from a very prestigious company, making about what I was at my last job. But, I turned it down because I wanted to give my own thing a full go. I look back now and I am amazed by the size of my balls and/or complete stupidity.

At this point I was working with veterans and attempting to build my business. If I'm being completely honest, I really had no idea what I was doing. I was doing the best that I could do with the information I had. I had a couple of really good people around me who provided a sounding board to keep me as stable as possible.

At home, it was just my golden retriever Leo and me, all by ourselves. The home that had once been the center of my family life had become a drab, quiet, empty house. I was left with basically nothing from the divorce. I had a mattress on the floor in my room. There was nothing on the walls and hardly anything in the kitchen. When people walked in the house it was if they paused and were like "whoa! It's sad in here!" I spent most of my time upstairs in my office, which was the one place I got to keep my

stuff. For me, that was the most normal place in the house. The rest of the house seemed like 2600 square feet of emptiness. I spent my evenings curled up in the bed with Leo watching TV. Most of my days, I did not even have direct interaction

with other human beings, since I mostly just communicated through the Internet and email. I would wake up, go upstairs, work all day, and then come down after dark. I would make a wrap or some sort of sad food and watch some Netflix with Leo.

Remember what "The Wizard" said? Don't make any big life decisions as you are going through a transition. I understand that sometimes it is unavoidable. However, if there is a way to avoid it I would say try if you can. It is such a volatile time where you are not thinking 100% clearly and more than likely your perception will change in the near future. I wasn't doing so well with this piece of advice myself. I'd changed jobs, gotten a divorce, started my own business and started a non-profit.

Around this time, I was realizing that I had more issues than just adapting to a new life. Now, I had taken some blows, but I was finally starting to feel somewhat normal or, at least, what I thought was normal at the time. I had recently hooked up with a friend who noticed some weird things about my daily behavior. He asked if I had had my testosterone levels checked. I had not, nor did I really know the impacts of low testosterone in men at the time. He made a recommendation to see his doctor and I went and saw him. As I mentioned earlier, I was at a 240, which is the level of a 72-year old man. Hell, I even know some 70-year old men with higher levels than that. The doctor immediately put me on a Hormone Replacement Therapy plan complete with vitamins and a diet. It drastically changed me for the better. Someone might think the stigma is true and that someone taking testosterone is "getting jacked up on steroids." However, do you know how I felt? Normal, just normal. I did not look like a bodybuilder and I did not get all ripped or started putting on a ton of muscle. What did start to happen was that my libido started to come back, I was recovering much better from training, my sleep started to improve, my mood started to get more positive, and I started to see a vision of where I wanted to go. Yet, something was still off.

During that time, there was a conference down in Tampa called the Special Operations Forces Care Coalition Annual Conference. Karl suggested that we would meet up and go down there for networking. It was a three-day conference with different speakers and panels discussing the problems that Special Operations Veterans were facing and what SOF CARE and other originations were doing to assist. During one of the presentations I saw Dr. Cagan

Randall get up and share a story about a MARSOC Marine who went through his facilities program. I just happened to know this Marine and was blown away by a couple of things. One: the fact that he had these issues that were so similar to mine. And two: that there was something that could be done about them. We were still in the beginning stage of my non-profit The Raider Project and I was just starting to figure out that our veterans did not necessarily need help with getting a good, high-paying job, but rather help with living a happy life. I was on a search for different options for our guys so I could help them be successful at life. But I did not want to subject my guys to hocus pocus or snake oil. I wanted something that actually worked. So I used myself as a guinea pig to find out if something was legitimate. All I had from the presentation was a link to a survey for veterans. So I filled it out in order to get more information so that I could provide that service to other vets.

Two days after I got back from my trip, I got a call from a lady at the brain clinic. She said, "Hi Nick, I got your survey and we were hoping you could get on a plane asap so that you could come through our program." I was pretty surprised since I didn't think there was anything wrong with me. I was just trying to get some info for my guys. Remember that time on the beach? The truth was, I was rapidly approaching that scenario again. My business was not growing, my house once filled with the laughter of my daughters was now empty and cold, I missed my kids, and I started to have all those old feelings of wasting my life and that everything was lie. I had made a mistake by getting out and I should have stayed in and kept deploying.

Anyhow, something in this screening I took definitely highlighted where I was at the given time and how many issues I was having. I did not go immediately, but we worked it out and I went pretty soon after that phone call. I won't bore you with the science of the whole thing, but essentially I had an undiagnosed Traumatic Brain Injury (TBI). There were in fact only two, well three, big instances that I remembered that could have caused this so I was shocked to hear this from Dr. Randall. One was an explosion in Iraq which I was not medevac'd for; it just rocked my world. Another was a vehicle incident in Afghanistan where I was thrown from an ATV like a dummy, not wearing a helmet at the time, and hurt my head. The last one was when my good buddy Josh and I were the Primary Safety Officers for an AT4 shoot. We took turns assisting people shooting these shoulder-fired rocket launchers. I think all and all we fired about 24 of them. Now, according to the Army Filed Manual 3-23-25: *"Within a 24-hour period, a soldier may only fire, observe fire, or act as safety NCO for the M136 AT4 one to three times, depending upon the firing position used."*

Needless to say Josh and I went over and above that number. I remember that my insides were vibrating and I felt all mushy inside after that day. I was nauseous and dizzy for about three days after that. We still laugh and shake our heads to this day over our stupidity and carefreeness.

Dr. Randall, the TBI expert, continued to ask me questions like how many parachute openings I'd had, how many flash bangs went off by my feet, how many door breaches I'd partaken in. His point was that all of these cause a little damage to the brain like chipping away at it one piece at a time. When I got there for my test I learned that one of my eyes was not in sync with the other, meaning if I looked left, my left eye would move, then milliseconds later my right eye would follow. With this going on all day long, it was no wonder I was getting motion sickness in a car, on a boat, sitting still. On top of that I failed my balance test. What? I failed my balance test? I went into that going: "Yea, I'm going to smoke this." You see, I'm a surfer, skateboarder, and snowboarder - I can balance. Yep, failed that one. He said that if he had not seen me in person and just looked at the results from the tests then he would have probably pegged me for an elderly person about to go on a walker.

I spent two full weeks at this clinic in Dallas, Texas going through all kinds of different exercises to get my brain firing the way it was supposed to. I'll tell you this: my first night after going through a full day of therapy I slept so hard. I fell asleep as soon as I got to my room and did not even move until it was time to get up and go back to the clinic. The Dr. also verified the issues with my hormones and concurred with my hormone doctor about the plan that I was on. Through these various injuries, my pituitary gland, which is the gland that regulates your hormones, had been damaged. Between that and the constant adrenaline spikes that Special Operators have for over a decade, my hormones were shot. This is something we see as a chronic issue in Special Operators and First Responders after over a decade of service.

He also gave me some news that I was not really stoked to hear: I had pre-Hashimoto's disease.

"Hashimoto's thyroiditis is an autoimmune disorder. These types of disorders are caused by a malfunction in your immune system. Doctors aren't sure what causes autoimmune disorders to occur. The main risk factor for developing Hashimoto's thyroiditis is having a pre-existing autoimmune condition, such as type 1 diabetes."

-Reference: Mayo Clinic

This is something that I was not really excited about because it's not easy to work around, but the reality was that I had to start making some different lifestyle choices if I did not want this to escalate and get worse.

After my time at the brain clinic in Texas I was on fire. I felt as if someone had given me the limitless pill. My brain had all these ideas, I was excited about life, and I definitely had a lot to live for. It was as if the fog in my brain had been cleaned out and I was thinking clearly and sharply for the first time since probably 2009. I went home with Leo and I started to get to work on my business and The Raider Project. I had such a clear vision that everything just started to happen. It was almost as if I would just touch something and it would turn to gold. Before it was as if I was walking through mud all the time and now I was running along with little resistance. I felt invincible and nothing could stand in my way.

I was not out of the woods yet despite this big leap forward. I had a lot of personal growth ahead of me. And I missed the heck out of my girls. I felt as if now I was ready and needed them to be back. I felt stupid for even letting them go so far away in the first place. As I said, I was not thinking clearly during my divorce. For anyone going through anything like this: do not under any circumstance let your children go. Hold them as tight as possible and get to work on being the best parent you can be because you need them just as much as they need you. If that means getting really vulnerable with yourself and what you need to be healthy then ruck up and do it. You will be the better for it in the long run.

As time went on, I realized that veterans' issues and my issues were not logistical in nature, meaning not an infrastructure problem. Most of these guys were talented and had the aptitude to do anything. We are highly capable individuals with a unique skill to blend into any environment and be successful. The issue was not that of finding a good job or networking correctly, the issue was their mental and physical health. Once we left the military, we were all going through an identity crisis in one way or another on top of having to deal with all the medical issues for the first time in our adult lives. I had an epiphany that if I could get a veteran healthy, whole, and stable then the infrastructure/logistical issues basically fixed themselves. Go figure, right? If I'm healthy, happy, and stable then life becomes easier… Not sure why this took me a couple of years to figure out.

Remember all that anger and bitterness I had? The more I worked on myself and the more I focused on my brain, my physical well-being, and mental health, the more whole and introspective I became. It was if I was finally figuring out who I was outside of the Marine Corps. I was dangerously close to becoming a "whole" human being. Through this process, I also realized that I couldn't be angry with the Marine Corps anymore. I was not a victim and no one owed me anything. Even if I had gotten screwed over, it was still my choice how I allowed it to affect me. Sure, I could go kick the can down the street cussing and yelling all the way down. But where is that going to get me? Is that going to make me happy? Am I going to feel better? Is that going to make my relationship with my daughters better? Is it going to make my business flourish? No, it will not and the sad point is you are the only one it's affecting. Do you really think the Marine Corps cares? Do you think the person who screwed you over way back when is staying up at night thinking about you? Nope... it is just your life that it's messing up at this point. I realized that people are going to do what they will to others out of their own insecurities. We screw each other over all the time. That's a sad fact of life and something we cannot control. What we can control is ourselves and how we allow it to affect us in OUR life. We are in control of our domain, our brain, our spirit, and our heart. We have the power to let others affect us in that way or not. That realization is powerful.

I was no longer mad at the Marine Corps. The Marine Corps mission is to have a force that is trained, organized and equipped for offensive amphibious employment and a "force in readiness." Nowhere in there was it ever implied that the Marine Corps mission was to make Nick Koumalatsos a good dad, human, or civilian. But somehow we hold the organization accountable for just that despite the fact that its sole mission is to fight and win our nation's battles.

Now, let me address this effort of putting the work in. First, let me ask you how long it takes for someone to become a Marine? How much training does it take to become a Marine Raider? How much money? I go to Marine Corps Recruit Training and spend 3 months (for me it was 5.5 months due to my dumbass breaking my wrist) to become a Marine. Then I go to more combat training, then I got to my occupational training. Then I get a hankering for more excitement, so I go Force Recon and train for almost 7 months to become a Reconnaissance Marine. Then I go to Jump School, SERE School, Combat Dive School, Shooting packages, patrol packages, and breacher packages. Then I go do the job on a handful of deployments around the globe and decide I'm going to become a Marine Raider with Marine Special Operations Command. Ok, now I'm going through Assessment and Selection, then more school, and more training. By the time I left MARSOC as a Marine Raider, they had millions of dollars invested in me for me to become a good Marine Raider with the experience and qualifications I needed to do my job. 12 years of training and deployments! Do you think you can go do all that and then one day flip a switch and be a good civilian? You put countless reps in pulling your pistol and practicing your marksmanship to be perfect. After all that muscle memory in every training or mission you have accomplished and you still think you are just going to flip that switch with the 5 days of our out-processing training that they give us and be good to go? Yea, because that equals out (said with the most sarcastic voice I can)!

If you want to be a good dad, then you have to put the effort and time in. It does not happen overnight. Just like if you want to be a good shooter, you have to put in the reps and put the bullets down range. It does not happen overnight. All of these take  work, practice and time. It is asinine to think that you can get away with not putting in the work for it and be good at something. This is true for being a civilian or whatever you need to be in the next chapter of your life, just like it was true for being a Marine or whatever you were before your life changed. You might be tempted to think that you are the exception to the rule and that you will just naturally be great at whatever life throws your way. However, chances are that you need to apply yourself and work hard to get to a point where you can feel good about yourself in a new life stage.

We don't just have to work hard though. We also have to put in recovery work. Most veterans train their bodies so hard. We will plan out our workout program down to the smallest detail, but we will not focus on recovery. Yet, recovery is how we actually get better. We have to develop a 1:1 ratio of work and recovery. You have to work hard to become great at your new life in your new chapter, but if you don't put the effort forth in being vulnerable with yourself and identifying your weaknesses, then you are going to be stuck and will not improve. Instead of getting you where you need to be in six months to two years, it might take a decade to get you where you need to be if you refuse to sit down and recover on a personal level.

What I started to not understand, even in myself, was the lack of willingness to deal with these personal issues. We come from this warrior mentality where we will go into close combat with and destroy the enemy by fire. We will do whatever it takes to complete the mission. I mean we will hail down fire, brimstone, and use whatever hate and discontentment we can find to crush the enemy that is in the way of our object. We are a force that is filled with so much piss, vinegar, and hate that nothing can stand in our way. But! When it comes to ourselves and having to look inward and deal with our fucking problems, that warrior turns into a little bitch. Why don't we attack our mental health recovery or our life problems with as much vigor and intensity as we do some foreign enemy? If we did I bet we would crush them just as easily as we crush our enemies.

We need to stop being bitches. We are not victims. We are not owed anything; the world does not owe us. We volunteered to do that job, most of us several times. We did it. And now it is up to us to make something of ourselves and be a warrior in this new world as we were when we were fighting a foreign enemy.

Now, you might not be a veteran, but I'm willing to bet that you can still find some use in this. Maybe you've found a new job, maybe you've gotten divorced, or maybe you've just started college. You thought life was going to be great and that you were going to rock it. But after going through all the bad emotions and feeling a bit depressed about life for reasons you don't really understand, you have finally decided that this needs to stop. This is where you need to sit down and get to work. You need to look at what issues you are having and take steps to deal with them. Is your apartment a sad mess after your wife left? Clean it up and organize it the way you want it! Are you constantly gaining weight because you don't know how to cook? Get a freakin' cookbook and find a helpful YouTube channel so that you can learn this basic life skill. For veterans and civilians alike, this stage is hard, but rewarding. It is all about 1) recognizing the issue, 2) developing an approach, and this might require finding an MD or calling an interior decorator and then 3) applying yourself to grow and move forward.

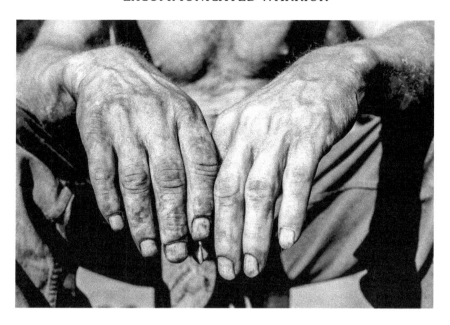

In other words, get your hands dirty and put the fucking work in!

STAGE 7: MAKING IT TO THE TOP

In the summer of 2016 I made my first attempt to summit Mount Rainier. I knew because of my schedule, money, and geographical location, I probably only had one shot at this. So knowing this, I put a plan into place. First things first: I had just been cleared on April 1 to start using my hand again after an injury I sustained while filming a show for the Discovery Channel. As Murphy's Law would have it, I went out to SLC to film a teaser for a veteran horseback trip we were planning.

During the filming I was bucked from the horse and I threw my back out and was hardly able to walk. I went home and saw the chiropractor three times a week for almost two months before it felt normal. Then I got the call that I had a spot on the trip to Mt Rainier. I had a little over three weeks to train. I knew that I was not in the physical shape that I should be, however, I knew that I could mentally go to a dark place and block out the pain to continue up the mountain. If my time in the Marine Corps with Marine Reconnaissance and Marine Special Operations had taught me anything, it is that I can endure a good amount of pain.

Since I knew I would be able to deal with the pain, I analyzed the situation and got to the conclusion that there was one thing that might prevent me from summiting: the altitude. I lived in North Carolina at sea level and I was about to attempt to summit the hardest endurance climb of the lower 48 states of the USA. The summit sits at 14,411ft or 4,392 m. At 8000 ft a person who is not acclimatized might start to have symptoms of altitude sickness. Because I was living at sea level, I knew that I would probably have some symptoms during the climb if I didn't take steps to prevent that. The main issue with altitude sickness is that if you get it while you are trying to summit you are pretty much done. The only way to fix it is to go back down. If you continue to go up, it will continue to get worse. This is one of the main causes that climbers aren't able to summit.

Being the good Operations Chief I once was, I wanted to mitigate the one thing that was out of my control. I rented an altitude training system from Hypoxico, complete with a tent and a mask to continue to train with. I started out at 8000 ft and worked my way up rapidly. I slept in the tent at 14,000 ft for almost three weeks while also training on my Stairmaster with the mask between 8000 ft and 14,000 ft, doing different interval training sessions on the Stairmaster as well as lots of Kettlebell work for conditioning. I know three weeks is not a long time, but it was the time that I had and I had to make every day count. I spent my last night in the tent at 14,000 ft, and then early that morning I boarded my flight to Seattle, Washington. I had to stay one night in Seattle, but I quickly left the city and went to sleep in a cabin up on the mountain so that I could get back up in the altitude. My second night was at 6000 ft and the next day I met up with the climbing team and we started our trek.

Guess what happened - I had no altitude issues because I had properly planned. And guess what else - it fucking hurt and just like I knew I could, I powered through the pain and put one foot in front of the other. One inch at a time until I crested that crater and put my name in that book on the top of that mountain. I had identified what I could control, what I could not, and what I could mitigate. I'll never forget our primary guide Dennis Broadwell telling my after the fact, "Yea man, I looked back and it looked like you went to a very dark place those last several hundred feet," to which I replied: "Yep!"

Now, did I leisurely get to the top of that mountain? Hell no! I had to take every painful step all the way to the top. I had to put in the work and put one foot in front of the other to get there. There were no shortcuts, no tips, no  easy way, just hard work and the time put in. And it felt damn good to say that I summited on my first attempt.

Okay, so we need to grab our ruck and get serious in our life as well. We need to get vulnerable, open up, and admit that we are having some issues with life and ourselves. We need to start to put the work in as if we were hiking a mountain. If you do it correctly, every day gets a little bit better than the day before as we apply ourselves and focus on the goal. Every week gets a little bit better until we are months into the process and we can actually breathe again. Life is not so bad - life is actually good. You will say to yourself: "I can't believe I was ever there and wanting to just end my life." At that point, it will feel like you have gotten to the top of your mountain. From there everything seems so clear. You can see further than you would have ever imagined possible; no more being in the fog and not knowing where to go, no more being in pain - it's all behind you. From up there you have the best seat in the house. You can pick any direction and know which way to go. Plus it's all downhill from there.

Unfortunately, that is not exactly the way life works, is it? At some point life is going to try its damnedest to kick us off that mountain. It could be a job, the economy, a friend or family member, a divorce, or even a natural disaster. My point is that life will continue to happen and we have to fight to stay on that mountain; we have to fight to be where we are because we fought to get there. It is ours, we earned it, and we are not going to let anyone take our growth and progress away from us.

Sometimes there are uncontrollable circumstances that we either can't prepare for or just don't see coming. When it comes to those times, we just have to roll up our sleeves and deal with it. Getting laid off because of downsizing, a spouse leaving you, getting injured - these are just a few things that we have to just process and deal with. We still should not quit and we should not give up or give in. As I said, we made it to the top of this freaking mountain and we are going to fight to stay there.

What I want to talk about are the things that are in our control. I have this talk regularly with a good buddy of mine about veterans having the ability to live a good life. There are many of them that think they can't. It is very sad and unfortunate that they believe that. It could not be farther from the truth. The issue is that they have some of the symptoms and issues we have discussed in prior chapters, but when asked what they are doing about it, they say that they honestly are not doing anything. They are just sitting on the couch every day with their smart phones, complaining about their problems to people. Woe-is-me nonsense. They don't realize that there are many things and problems that they can control. If you've identified that you have a drinking issue because you use it to cope with your problems, then maybe you should not be hanging out at a bar every night until midnight. My point is that anyone and everyone can live a good life. Your life just might not look like your neighbor's or your best friend's version of a good life. Maybe you have sleep issues and your nighttime routine is set in a way that allows you to get the best sleep possible, so you can wake up the next day happy, refreshed, and ready to kick the day in the shin. So, while your co-workers or friends are going out having drinks late after work, you go home and stick to your routine because that is what keeps you on your mountain.

I believe everyone can live a great life after a traumatic event or a big life transition. I just believe it won't necessarily look like the life everyone else is living. You own it 100%. If you don't live it for you, everyone around you will suffer as much as you do.

What staying on top of my mountain means for me is that I go to bed and get good sleep. I don't stay up late, I do yoga, I meditate, I get in the water, I maintain my physical fitness, and I don't eat like an asshole. It means I show more love and it means I'm vulnerable with those that I love and care about. That is how my life has to be for me to stay on top of my mountain. Now, I understand that you may look around you and see people that just kind of float through life with no routine or things that keep them anchored. That is fine. But I have to keep reminding myself that that is not me. If I don't focus on myself and the things that keep me whole, those things that keep me on my mountain, then I will fall down several hundred feet and have to work even harder to get back up. And to be honest, I know what it feels like to begrudgingly climb back up because you've forgotten how to stay on top. I finally know what it takes and the things that I should and shouldn't be doing. It's a long process to figure out exactly what this life looks like for you. There is a lot of trial and error. But it's worth it to get to wake up to that beautiful view from the top of the mountain every day.

If I do the things I need to do I am beyond happy with my life, and I'm more productive every day. I can honestly equate me doing these things with the success that I have had in my life, relationships, and my businesses. Yep, that is right. I now have five businesses on top of being the Director for The Raider Project. It's amazing what you can accomplish when you are healthy, stable, and on top of the mountain with a clear view of the world.

This is where Miss Capra enters the picture. When the stars line up just right you meet someone who lights your whole world on fire. Someone that enhances your life and doesn't detract from it. An individual who lifts you up when you're down, or maybe even humbles you a little bit when you get too full of yourself. If you ever find a rad chick that is like that, strap on boys because you are in for the ride of your life. Now with all that said, I think the truth is that every dude wants a rad chick until he has a rad chick! Things are never dull!

It took a couple of years for me to climb my mountain and get to a good place in my life. And through this time, I was fortunate enough to find a woman who complemented my personality and future goals. That person we all strive to find to share a life with. That connection that you get and realize that you had been missing a piece all along. The person who sees you for who you are going to become and helps you become that person. I have to say I was fortunate enough to find her and keep her as I worked through my transition. I don't want you to think this is a book about relationships. This book is about YOU! We have to have our shit together before we get into a relationship.

If you happen to meet someone while you are going through all this, you need to do a self-evaluation on the situation and the person. Is this person going to assist and be a positive influence that helps you reach or keep you on the top of your mountain, or is she going to light your house on fire and watch it burn? Because all too often what happens is that a person will meet another person and their goals and ideals don't match. That relationship will keep you from staying on your mountain. The fallout from this is very bad and can take months/years to repair. Too often men in our position sabotage themselves with chaos, sometimes in the form of a crazy chick. Remember that your number one responsibility is to yourself. It is imperative that we remain healthy and stable because when we are, everyone around us benefits: our significant others, our children, our co-workers, our employees. But the minute we start to fall off the wagon the same applies: you suffer and everyone around you will suffer as well. So you need to seriously evaluate who you are deciding to attach to this journey and consider the fact that they might not want to sign on to what you are going through at the moment.

Lucky for me, a pretty girl found me and she wanted to climb with me. Miss Capra saw me for who I was, she saw the baggage I was carrying, she saw the pain from my past and she wanted to help me move forward. She made lists for me of things I was passionate about, she kept me on a healthy routine, hell, she even rubbed my feet until I fell asleep on some nights. We set goals together, we journal, we travel, we experience, we live. I have never felt so supported in my whole life. And that has definitely been a positive factor in my recovery and my ability to stay on top of my mountain.

Another important factor in my life is my family. During this time, I finally got my daughters back. The way we had set things up was not working for the girls and their mother. We felt that co-parenting in a location that everyone felt familiar with would be best for everybody. Those months when my girls were gone were

some of the worst months of my life. Worse than firefights, worse than deaths, worse than anything I'd ever experienced. I could not handle being away from my girls. And this was different from being deployed. Being without them in an empty house with a mattress on the floor was different. It was so quiet it hurt. I wanted to be with them. They were and still are my world. After all, my family was one of the main reasons why I got out in the first place. They were the whole reason I did not accept the civilian jobs deploying overseas basically doing the same thing I had been doing in the Marine Corps just as a government contractor. I wanted to be there for them and I almost messed that up. But they were back, and I was going to put in the work to re-establish those relationships that I had formed so long ago when they were little with every day off, every leave block, every dad-daughter date. After all the work put in to get me where I was, I was not going to fail them. Miss Capra and I went to Ikea and got all new furniture for their room since it was empty. We painted the walls, ripped the carpet out, put down new faux wood floor, and installed all the new furniture. They had a loft bed system with a living room and desk below. I was pretty proud of it. We even decorated the room with all their favorite superheroes.

Once we got all settled I wanted to have a serious talk with my daughters, one that I knew was going to be difficult, although I did not realize how difficult it would actually be. So here was the objective: getting all the problems out in the open and dealing with them. I got a whiteboard and we were going to take turns writing down all the events that we had experienced as difficult or hard on us as a family. So, for the next thirty minutes the three of us took turns writing down events that were hard on us. I was not prepared for what was happening. We were in tears. The whiteboard was completely filled to the point that we had to write in the small, little white space between the lines. Things like words that were spoken too harshly, someone was made fun of for a stance they were taking on a subject, the constant separations and fights with their mom (they actually thought all of our separations were divorces, they thought we had been divorced 4 different times and that really broke my heart), and me being deployed for months and months. It might not seem like much, but when you are sitting in a room looking at your two precious, little girls, who you love more than anything on the planet, writing such events down and reflecting on the hardest things they had ever experienced, with tears in their eyes - that has a heavy impact on you. After we were done writing all the hard things down, the next step was to talk them through ALL of this emotional duress and to help them understand one VERY big idea. I told them this: "WE have been through all of these hard things, and guess what… WE are still HERE!" I wanted them to know that the three of us had been through hard things and that we would continue to do so. That we as a family could get through anything. The Koumalatsos can do hard things. THIS was quite possibly one of the hardest and most rewarding things I have ever done with my girls. After all the tears, after all the talking, BOTH of my girls just wanted me to hold them. We just sat there together, wiped our tears, and mounted the board on the wall as a reminder that we were going to be ok. About six months later the girls asked if they could put the board away. They said they felt like they were ready to move past it. Things with the divorce had been hard. Because I had been deployed so much while they were so young, it was as if the girls felt like they had to "choose sides." After we did this whiteboard exercise, it was like they weren't afraid anymore. We got closer and closer every day and things felt normal again. Maybe even better than normal actually. The point of this story is to highlight how I had to get vulnerable and open with my daughters in order to put some work in and grow with them and our relationship. I don't know if this tool is right for you and your family, but I am telling you that you've got to get vulnerable, in order to really MAKE IT TO THE TOP.

I want to leave you with another story about putting the work in. As I continued to help veterans, I received more and more phone calls from veterans telling me about all their problems. The conversation would often go something like this:

Veteran: "My wife sucks, my kids suck, my job sucks. I can't sleep, I am unmotivated, and honestly my life just sucks!"

Me: "Okay"

Veteran: "Yea man, everything is fucked up,"

Me: "Okay, so what are you actually doing?"

Veteran: "Me? I'm mostly sitting on the couch."

Me: "Okay, but you have all these issues, what are you doing about them?"

Veteran: "Well... Nothing..."

Me: "So your car is on the side of the road with a flat tire, are you just going to sit there and complain about it?"

Veteran: "Well no... I would get out and change it."

Me: "So then do something, get off the couch, and change your freaking tire!"

What I'm saying is that if there is a problem then you need to do something about it. I promise you that doing nothing and putting zero effort into something will get you just that - NOTHING! However, on the flip side, if you work your ass off and put the effort into everything you are doing, you will see an exponential return of investment. I'm not going to say you won't fail as long as you put in the work. You absolutely will fail from time to time, but that is how you learn. Show me someone successful and I'll show you how that exact same person has failed 15 times to have the one success that you see. Nothing happens overnight - it all takes time and failures. So if you have to fail 15 times to get that one successful story, then you better get to work and start failing fast and often because the sooner you do, the sooner you will get to the success.

I feel like I have failed so much it is almost a joke amongst close friends. I would try anything because I got to a place where I realized there was a clock that I was working with. I figured that as long as I worked my ass off and kept moving forward I would be successful. I just had to go through all the failures first, which I did. I failed as a parent countless time. I failed at relationships both past and present. I epically failed at my business countless time and wasted thousands of dollars that I would know how to flip into a profit now if I only had known a fraction of what I now know. I failed my body so much that it revolted against me. All of these failures I had to come to terms with and learn from. I am better, stronger, and smarter because of them.

Here is the common denominator throughout this stage: I Never Quit, I Never Surrendered, and I Always Move Forward.

3 STEPS TO HAPPINESS
RECIPE FOR SUCCESS

Yep, that is correct. I have three steps to happiness and I'm going to give them to you right now: all you have to do to be successful and happy is to get a good night's rest, aka sleep, be healthy, and find your passion. I'm not the smartest guy in the world (#notadoctor) and I'm halfway kidding when I try to simplify success and happiness in life like that, but it's actually extremely effective if you follow these three steps. It sounds too easy to really matter, but even though these steps seem small each step can feel like an insurmountable mountain for anyone who is struggling to get his or her life back together.

I left active duty service and checked in to my Veterans Affairs Clinic since that is where I would be receiving my healthcare for the remainder of my life. Anyone who has done this knows that when you check in, you get what I like to call the VA starter kit. This kit includes all the bare necessities to function as a human being post-military service, or, in my words, to turn you into an absolute zombie and possibly kill you. When I checked in without hardly even speaking to anybody, they prescribed me Ambien for sleep, Prazosin for bad dreams, Zoloft for depression and anxiety, Adderall for focusing at work, and Tramadol for pain management. All at once and to be taken daily. Looking back at this, I'm completely dumbfounded that this even happened. If you have ever met anyone that is taking the VA starter kit as prescribed, you would be blown away at how they behave. It is like speaking to a zombie or someone that is so out of touch with reality it seems they are in another universe. Needless to say, that's not a long-term solution for anyone.

Unfortunately, this is not only an issue at the VA. Almost any person with a Primary Care Physician can go to him or her, explain the personal issues he or she is dealing with, and get all of the same medications dropped on them with just a mention of a few symptoms of mental instability. I'm sure we all know someone who is using some or all these medications or has in the past. A stay-at-home mom goes to the doc and says: "I'm really depressed and getting a ton of anxiety trying to manage my family." Boom! She has a Zoloft prescription in hand as she walks out the door and she can pick it up at the nearest pharmacy on the way home. It is sad to say, but the majority of doctors in this day and age is just treating the symptoms instead of diving down and revealing the root of the problem. It is much easier to swallow a small blue pill to suppress those symptoms than to put the dirty, hard, and vulnerable work in required to get to the root of the issue.

It's important to understand that in some situations that medication can provide life-saving relief in a very intense situation and I would never look down on or judge anyone for having to use medications as a temporary means of therapy. I just don't believe it's the long-term solution.

I was going through one very rough patch during my transition where I thought the entire world was out to get me. At this point, one of the pills I had never taken was the Zoloft. For some reason, I thought it was crazy to take that although I had no issues using the other ones in the past. Now, the "Doctor of Medicine", the MD, is a psychiatrist who prescribes you pills. This person is not your therapist. They simply go down a checklist and ask you generic questions. Based off your responses and past medical record they prescribe you medication to assist with whatever symptom you are experiencing. I tell you this because the same MD that prescribed my Zoloft, prescribed all of the other drugs, too. This doctor specifically told me to take the Zoloft at night with my Lunesta in the evening and it would just assist in relaxing me and would help me sleep. She was 100% correct - it would assist me in sleeping all the way into the grave. I took this pill one night and it would be the first and last time. As I said, I was having a rough go and just wanted a little help while I dealt with some of my personal issues. As I lay down and started to fall asleep that night I started to have trouble breathing. I was slowly going into respiratory arrest. As if that was not bad enough, the Zoloft mixed with my sleep medicine was making me pass out and fall asleep. This triggered a mild anxiety attack. All I could think was that I was going to die in my sleep just like two other Marines that had recently passed away from a bad mixture of prescription drugs issued by the VA. I was trying my best to breathe and not fall asleep because I felt that if I were to fall asleep that would have been it for me. Thankfully for me Miss Capra was there and got me to pound water and worked on calming my heart down which helped to get my breathing under control. I had never felt so out of control of my own body before. And it was simply a negative reaction to medication. The next day we looked up those medications and it was plain as day that they should never be taken together. When I went to see the MD, she simply shrugged her shoulders, let out a nervous giggle and said: "Well, that shouldn't have happened. I guess we won't do that again." I just sat there with my mouth wide open. I haven't been back ever since.

Now, let's get to work on the three steps. I know I said three steps and we will start with sleep because we have to start somewhere, but all three of these steps are dependent on each other. So, while finding your passion might be a bit off in the beginning, you can still start working on that step or hell, your passion at this step might just be going the fuck to bed! This is something I certainly had to learn how to do. As I said previously, we work so hard in the gym to get all jacked, tan, and ripped, but when it comes to recovery and sleep we just expect it to naturally/organically happen. Wrong! We have to build the muscle memory to make it happen just as if we were shooting on the gun range.

SLEEP

I had stopped sleeping through the night in 2009 while I was in Afghanistan. I can't tell you why or that I really even noticed it fully at first. I guess I just chalked it up to being on deployment and sleeping in less than desirable conditions, not having a regular sleep schedule, or, hell, maybe I was just getting older. On top of those considerations, there were also the aggressive firefights I was experiencing in my dreams, to the point that my blood pressure would elevate and I would wake up in cold sweats. The issue was that when I came home it did not improve. Besides from dreaming about fighting, I started having nightmares about men I watched die. Whenever I did fall asleep, I would sleep very lightly and was easily woken up to any little movement or noise. This just became the new normal. As the years and sleepless nights rolled by during my time as a Marine, the ever increasing intake of alcohol just seemed to be a natural occurrence because it would get me to wind down and go to sleep. Then once I got out of the military, I needed both sleep meds and booze to help the situation.

What happens to the human body when we don't sleep for a prolonged period of time? I can speak from my own experience from going through Recon Indoctrination Platoon (RIP) as I made my way into the Reconnaissance community. We were conducting our Patrol Phase in RIP. This is where you patrol every night conducting various Reconnaissance missions with your team. The "fun" part of this is that you don't sleep at all that week. You plan during the day and execute very long and strenuous patrols at night conducting those missions. No big deal, right? After all, this is Force Recon training - time to man the F up! While there is some truth to that, your body and mind are not always on the same page as you when it comes to going without sleep for a long time. The common trend we see with these training operations is that the guys start to get a little loopy around the third night of no sleep. I'll never forget my third night in my RIP Patrol phase. I was the Assistant Team Leader (ATL) on this patrol and it was about 2am as we were about halfway done with the mission when I started to hallucinate. Yep, I was straight up seeing shit in the woods that wasn't there. As I continued to check the route we had just walked for security purposes, as an ATL does, I started to see military service members following us. But something was different; they were all Vietnam-era Marines. The old steel bucket helmets, with cut-off sleeves, wearing old-school style gear, called 782 gear or Deuce Gear. This continued for a minute until I looked back one more time and I saw a Marine on all fours with Garfield sitting on his back licking his paws. Yep, Garfield the cat! A freaking cartoon character. I rubbed my eyes and that was the moment I knew I was just a little bit tired. Now, there are some training objectives behind the sleep deprivation when you are going through a course like this, but my point is that it deeply affects the human body to go without sleep for whatever reason.

With lack of sleep, you can expect to be tired during the day, experience a lack of energy, depression, anxiety, irritation, anger, and it will affect your performance at work or school. It basically will turn you into a grump on a short-term basis, but worse still is that it can have seriously negative effects on your mental health long-term. You will stop thinking clearly and could even start to get paranoid. I have met people who have been struggling with insomnia for years and have developed paranoid disorder because of that. After we at the Raider Project get them the help they need and they start to sleep for the first time in years, they become like new people.

In order to find happiness you need to build a sleep routine. You need to train your body to the fact that it is time to rest at a certain time every night. I'll never forget when I met Miss Capra and she started to put all this alternative stuff (what I called Snake Oil) on me at bedtime. Right around bedtime she would put lavender essential oil on my neck and wrist. Supposedly, lavender essential oil helps to reduce stress and anxiety plus it helps to induce sleep. Another positive side effect of building a routine this way was that it was essentially building a Pavlovian response in me, which basically meant that I was being conditioned to getting tired when I smelled that smell and I actually started to get tired because the only time my brain experienced that smell was right before bed. Miss Capra knew what she was doing. As time went on, I would immediately feel less stressed and more relaxed when I smelled lavender, and it also made me think about her.

As human beings we are more in tune with the sun than we know. Have you ever been camping and when the sun goes down, you automatically start to get tired. The only light you have is the fire you made next to your tent. You yawn and go jump in your sleeping bag to fall right asleep and then you wake up when it starts to get light outside. The same would happen for me in Afghanistan. We would be out in some village, harbored up in a compound for the night and as soon as the sun went down I was ready to rack out and would be up at first light. I suggest attempting to implement a version of this in your sleep routine if you are struggling with insomnia. When the sun starts to go down, don't just flip every light on in the house. Maybe even get some dimmers so that you can turn certain lights on but keep them just bright enough to see what you are doing. You see one of the reasons we get tricked to stay awake is all the blue light from electronics and light bulbs that we subject ourselves to at nighttime. The sun goes down and now that we live in modern times we can crank on some lights, our TV, laptops, and our smart phones to keep that energy rolling. All of these omit blue light that stimulates our brains to think that it is still daytime. Then, despite the fact that it's late, our body thinks it still light out and it goes: oh shit, we need energy to stay awake! Let's crush some sugar and get this glycogen party rolling! Hence the reason you get a sweet craving late at night when you stay up.

I got some Hue bulbs by Philips so I could dim all the lights in the house at dusk and that allowed me to ease into my rest time. We killed the blue light, too. Most new smartphones and laptops have a feature where you can turn off the blue light so we did that. Then the TVs are turned off and it is time to wind down. Whether it is getting your journal out and journal at the end of the day in order to prep your calendar for the next day, jotting down some ideas you have been coming across throughout the day, or maybe it's reading a few pages in your favorite book, you need to get your mind to calm down without electronics. Once the lights are down I typically like to take a warm shower in the low light. Miss Capra will usually come in and toss some lavender over the shower door just to ensure the party is officially started. I then use my electric toothbrush and brush my teeth. I turn on my floor fan for noise, and then I crawl into bed. If I have done all my steps right from start to finish, it takes about 45 minutes, but I will fall asleep within 5 minutes of turning the lights fully off. Another thing you have to think about is that if you want to ensure that your entire body and mind are stimulated and flooded with adrenaline at bedtime. Then watch Die Hard before you lay down. You will be ready to go, but not to bed. You will not be ready to go to bed at all. Remember not to watch action movies or play video games before bed. If you're struggling with sleep, then you need to think about little things like this, or you will be tossing and turning all night.

But just like anything else, this is not an overnight solution. You do all this to build muscle memory. The bedtime routine will not work the first time, second time, or maybe even third. You have to put in the work and build the discipline to apply it every single night. Remember when I told you that you can have a happy life, but yours might just be different from others - this is what I was talking about. If you want it to work, you have to put the effort in to get the benefit. Do you think Mr. Olympia got on stage and won that title by half-assing it? No, he showed up to the gym every day, built a routine and worked his ass off. You will have to apply yourself at your sleep hygiene and routine. I promise you that once you get it down you will know how beneficial it is. I immediately know when I slack off by how I feel and how I perform. Sometimes, I will think something along the lines of: "I'm doing so much better, I don't need to do all that; I feel great!" Then I'll have a shitty week and realize what I've done to myself. I get right back to it and I'm all good.

At this point your whole mission in life might just be prepping yourself to get a good night's rest. When I was in this phase, this is basically what my day revolved around. I made sure to not have any sort of stimulants after 3pm, and I made sure that I got enough exercise first thing in the morning. And I had all of my tasks done before the sun went down. All of these things teed me up so that I could conduct my nightly routine and go to bed effectually. This wasn't particularly sexy. But it was what I needed. And still what I need to stay on my mountain.

GET HEALTHY AND FIT

The second thing you need to focus on is your overall health and fitness. This one can be a hard one for most of us. For some reason a lot of veterans attempt to compete with the physical version of themselves in the past. When I left the service, I was still training as if I was in Bala Murghab, Afghanistan with Marine Special Operations Team (MSOT) 8222.

Despite the physical and medical issues I had at the time, I was still trying to train as if I was on a team. I over-trained to the point that I was tearing tissue in my back and shoulders plus I was making what injuries I already had even worse. And to be completely honest, I did this with little to no return. I had no idea why I was training the way I was other than the fact that this was the only way I really knew how to train. It was the way I had trained for so long and I thought it was just the way it was done. I had to get to a place where I realized that I was training for life, my life, and no one else's. I had to stop competing with an older version of myself and start figuring out how to be the healthiest and fittest version I could be today. I had to find out what fit meant outside the world of the Marine Corps.

The truth is – I wasn't very healthy during my time as an active duty Marine either. I always wanted to be the most jacked and ripped guy on the team - we all did. So, the bigger I could be, the better. The more I weighed, the more I could lift, and the faster my sprint, the better. Regardless of the damage it was doing to me long term, I just wanted to be faster, stronger and bigger. I was trying to be the guy weighing in at over 230 at 6 feet. Don't get me wrong, I could still do 20 dead hangs, and run 7-minute miles, but I essentially had no need to carry that kind of weight around. What I should have been focusing on was my health, my endocrine system (hormones), my body fat, my diet, my mobility, and my recovery.

After years of constant pains and the realization that I had somehow gotten older, I finally arrived at a place where I was ready to get healthy. I had to get my testosterone in order, which I did. I had to start focusing on recovery mobility, how my body moved, and my flexibility. That is still something I struggle with today. The reason why I struggle is that I have gotten injured so many times and that hinders free movement in those areas of the body so they become tight and stiff. That ends up creating muscle pain and tightness. However, if we can get limber, more flexible and more mobile, our pain will significantly decrease. It was a big eye opener for me when it came to yoga. I had finally met some Marines that had adopted yoga as part of their recovery/practice and they had great results, not only with their physical joint pain and immobility but also their minds. Whenever you look at an older person who is hunched over and has bad mobility, you know that it is only a matter of time before they won't be around anymore. They end up with walkers, then in wheel chairs, just waiting on death. Yet, we see people like Mark Sisson, 65, Loren Cordain, 67, Arthur De Vany, 81, and my Doc, Dr. Robert Battmer, who all are in damn near better shape than me. There is a common theme: they walk a lot, they eat right, they balance their hormones, and they get a shit ton of sleep.

Once I got my shit together I dropped down to a healthier weight. That made my mobility so much better. I was able to hike faster, rock climb better, surfing was easier and I could last longer in general. I just felt better all-around. You don't have to be an athlete, like the next Olympian or CrossFit competitor. You just need to be better than you were the day before and put the effort forth. That might mean just starting to walk 15 minutes a day, then 30 minutes a day, then make it an hour. Maybe work out for 30 minutes in a gym, three days a week. These are all arbitrary recommendations, but my point is to just start. Just start somewhere!

There is more to health than just being in good shape though. When I went to the Brain Clinic they did a cortisol test on me. A cortisol test basically tells you how stressed you are. But, it did not only show how stressed I was, it also showed the spikes of my stress. The test came back and showed me that my stress spikes in the morning. So, Dr. Randall told me it would be best if I did my cardiovascular training first thing in the morning, around 6am. A cardio workout would crush that cortisol for the rest of the day. So, instead of spiking early in the morning and taking all day to come down, it would attempt to spike, but my physical output would crush the cortisol spike and it would remain at a lower level all day.

What is great when you start to train again is the dopamine release we get with exercise. Have you ever started a workout program and within a few weeks looked in the mirror with your shirt off and gone, "Damn, I'm looking good." I hate to break it to you, but you probably don't look much different. But seriously, I'm proud of you! We all do this. Hell, I do this! But the reason why we are starting to feel that way is that we get that dopamine release when we start to train so we feel better and more positive about our bodies and ourselves. I'm not talking about doing some crazy training where you are throwing up in a trashcan at the end of it. That is not proper training and if you get signed up for something like that you are heading in the wrong direction. Training like that will stress your body out and you don't need that. I'm talking about proper workout programs that slowly increase your physical capacity and strength. Even as soon as you have had one good training session, you are getting the hormone dopamine released in your system. Dopamine is the feel-good hormone. This is what makes us feel happy and confident.

Now you've addressed your hormones, your mobility, and your training. One thing is left: your diet. I'm not going to waste your time talking about healthy eating. You probably know what you're supposed to eat. Stay away from the daily donuts. Don't fuel up on gallons of coffee. Get plenty of vegetables, fruit, and meats. Take it easy when it comes to alcohol. You don't need to be a professional chef to pull this off.

We ran a program in North Carolina with The Raider Project where we would bring veterans in that needed to get out of their current situation and needed a change of perspective. We would put them on a very strict schedule of training, physical therapy, decompression therapy, and counseling. Their meals were catered from a healthy meal prep company locally. When they showed up they would be sad-looking zombies, dragging their feet along, and with no spark. However, within just two days of training and running on a strict schedule, and then passing out at the end of the night, they would be smiling and excited for every day ahead. Now, we did not have anything that they did not. We just put the routine and schedule in place for them and that was all they needed.

So start eating healthy - stop eating the shit that comes in a box and start eating real food. Start exercising - it can be push-ups, pull ups, and squats for 30 minutes a day, go walk to the end of your street, I don't really care. Just do something and make it a routine that you stick to.

FINDING YOUR PASSION

The final step for you is to find your passion. Now, this is easier said than done and your passion could drastically change as you go through your life, but this step is the difference between you being happy and you being unsatisfied for the rest of your life. If you choose your passion correctly you will live a very happy and fulfilled life. Now, I might lose some of you here because we are going to discuss what you want to do versus what you need to do. What I needed to do was get a job to continue the quality of life and standard that my family had been used to all of those years before I transitioned out of the military. What I probably should have done was take off to Greece for 6 months, like the Wizard said, to figure my shit out. At this point you might say something like, "Nick, that's just not a possibility for me." Is it really not? Or is the problem that it just does not fit in your life's current infrastructure. When we first look at the possibility of doing what we want versus what we are supposed to do, we try to fit our new life in with our old one. So you can't do what you want because you have all these bills and responsibilities lingering from your old life. What about those two cars? Can you go down to one? Ali and I sold one of our vehicles, so I have a vehicle for myself and Ali to get around, and a vehicle for my oldest daughter to get to and from school, work and both parents' homes. We make this work because we don't need extra vehicles sitting in our driveway. What about that 2500 square foot home? Can you go down to a 1200 square foot home if your kids share a bedroom? You might be asking, "Why on earth would I

do that?" What if I told you, you would actually be happier with less stuff and more freedom to do what you love? I know it's a crazy thought and it takes huge, brass balls to drastically change your life like that. But what if I told you that that was the only thing standing in your way of reaching your dreams and truly being happy?

People watch YouTube videos of Miss Capra and me gallivanting around the country. But guess what we don't spend money on - expensive handbags, name brand clothing, monstrous electronics, fancy dishes or new furniture. We have one normal-size TV that I've had for 10 years. We have had the same old furniture we bought at a garage sale years ago. Instead of spending our money eating lunch out every day, we prep food on the weekends and eat most of our meals at home. We don't have weekends to ourselves. We work all the time. We have multiple streams of income to support our life. We manage properties, which means leaving to sort out missing keys in the middle of the night or cleaning up messes we didn't make. The point is this: in order to live the life you've always wanted you must make sacrifices and sometimes give up convenience and comfort in exchange for adventures and new experiences. Maybe you don't want to travel and that's ok too. Your life will not look like mine and it shouldn't. It should look like the life you always wanted. There are plenty of ways to do what you love, but it may take you some creative maneuvering to seize those opportunities.

For most of my life I could not even imagine the possibility of doing what I wanted to do because of all my responsibilities: the kids had school, I had a mortgage, I had two car payments, I had a motorcycle payment, and the list went on. Never once did I consider the fact that we could move, we could get rid of a vehicle, and I never questioned if I really NEEDED a motorcycle, or if it was in the way of my dreams. I was trying to figure out how to get what I wanted without changing my life drastically, and that simply didn't work. If we are going to work towards our dreams and our passion, we are going to have to make sacrifices. Anything actually worth something is worth hard work and sacrifice. Otherwise it would not mean anything in the end. If any regular man that wanted an Olympic gold medal could get one, it wouldn't mean anything. It would kind of suck! Why are people so stoked and emotional when they receive an Olympic medal? It's because of the years of hard work and sacrifice it took to get there.

I'm sure if you think about it you can find the first 20 stories of people you know that went out on a limb to follow their passion. One of the stories that comes to mind for me was a family that started a gym. The parents both had good jobs with amazing benefits and salaries. However, they were not passionate about what they were doing. They came to the decision to open a gym because that was their passion; they wanted to help others and build up a community around working out. As I said, decisions like that one comes with sacrifices. They had to go down to one car, they had to get rid of their home and had to live in a room in the gym. Because of their schedule they had to home-school their kids. But guess what happened? They were happy! Were they rolling in money at first? Hell no! They were hardly making ends meet. But every month got a little better until now when they are living the life that they had always wanted and making it work for them.

Finding your passion is not something you do by following a direct line. In fact, it looks more like a 3-year old's drawing of a treasure map. Your first passion might be just trying to sleep better so that you can feel better. Your whole mission in life becomes figuring out how to go to bed in the right way so that you can get into that wonderful REM sleep and feel your body recover. Once you tackle that your next passion might be to become as physically fit and healthy as you can be. Once you have done that, the search begins as you start to figure out what you want to do with your life. There are not direct routes to this and you will find that nothing stays the same throughout this quest to find your passion. Life changes, we change, and that is okay.

When I left my career as a Marine Raider I did what I thought I was supposed to do. I did what every good Special Operator does and that's getting a job as a government contractor doing basically the same thing I had been doing my whole life, but now as a civilian. When that job ended I did what every Special Operator does when they are done contracting and that's to start a tactical consultation business. So I did that... I never stopped to ask if this was something I wanted. I never stopped and asked myself if I even liked doing what I was doing.

It wasn't until Miss Capra showed up and observed me working 80 hours a week to grow my first business that I even realized that what I was doing wasn't working. She said watching me stand on a 15ft fire line and teach people how to aim a firearm at a paper plate-size target was like watching me die a little every day. I have to admit, I hated it. The idea of building a business, an infrastructure, and a successful team made me excited, but the idea of watching myself dig berms, and spend my weekends on a riding lawn mower in the swamp sort of sounded like a death sentence.

Now, I don't want you to take this the wrong way - I love close-quarter tactics and personal security and teaching people how to be prepared for a home invasion. I actually first met Miss Capra because she put together a pistol course in Kansas City and I came to teach it. She's personally been through all my firearms training (carbine, pistol, CCH) because she loves that stuff and she wasn't trying to pull me away from it. She just noticed something very interesting at my first SMOKECHECK course. What is SMOKECHECK? I am glad you asked. You see, I realized what was missing from typical tactical handgun and marksmanship courses: stress. Anyone can stand on a line and hit a target, or even make it through a high-paced drill. But it is something else to be aiming and shooting a firearm while running from an enemy, being shot at and trying to pull dead (injured) weight. I wanted to create a course that gave civilians real life scenarios to sharpen their skills. What would you do if you were in a parking lot and you were being attacked? How would you actually get to your handgun and protect yourself? What if there were multiple attackers? My instructors and I created multiple scenarios and taught very intense techniques to train in these stressful scenarios. The course also included escape and evasion skills, survival skills (how to get clean water, make fire, etc.) and most importantly basic medical care for an active shooter scenario. The final day of the course we put it all into practice, we built teams and the instructors came full force against the students. Everyone was in the woods, in full gear, fighting to save their own lives and the lives of everyone on their team. It was amazing watching everyone pull together to protect one another. And honestly, I didn't realize how emotional it would make some of them. It was here Miss Capra had an epiphany. She saw me creating scenes, directing action, heck, even building a set for all the drama to take place. "You're a producer," she said. "You weren't meant to teach this, you were meant to create this." She had long told me that I was more creative than I ever gave myself credit for, and when she watched my eyes light up at the fruition of this course, it became even clearer to her. Even more so, I know exactly how I wanted her to shoot the whole thing and make it into a mini-movie when she did her marketing material for the company. She knew it wasn't the tactics I loved, it was the production. I was on my way to discovering what my passion was.

Fast forward a few months and a production company reached out to me wanting me to star in a show they were producing called "Trailblazers." It was a scripted reality show that featured former Special Operations guys leading a team of scientists into various locations to complete a scientific mission. I initially thought that was totally ridiculous. However, if it worked out for me to participate then that would be a lot of press and eyes on me which would hopefully trickle down to my business. Things continued to progress with the production company and it got more serious. They sent me a 21-page document to fill out that was about 90% essay questions. I was immediately out since I figured I had a business to run, a nonprofit to handle, and I was a single dad. It was not a priority for me at that point and seemed like too much of a hassle. So Miss Capra snatched my computer, filled the whole thing out, and submitted it. Boom! I got the job.

My mission was to escort a team of scientists to the deep Amazons of Bolivia to find an ancient black Cayman that had been isolated from the rest of the world for millions of years thus keeping it from evolving and adapting to new environments. This meant it was the closest thing to a dinosaur that we had on earth. Or something like that. When the scientists spoke it was a bit confusing. I just nodded and smiled and was the guy to get them in and get them out. Keep in mind that this is a television show and I mean a show. NOT reality! I linked up with the cast and crew in Miami and then we flew to Bolivia. Once we got our gear sorted out we started to shoot the series. When I tell you to find your passion, I hope your passion hits you so hard in the face that it is undeniably clear. That's how it was for me. I fell in love with the whole thing: getting the shots, performing, telling the story, all of it was exciting and so much fun. The first day the producer and director allowed me to assist them with the direction of shots for the series, almost as if I was also their on-set advisor. I actually saved two of the cast members from nearly drowning during a scene we were shooting in a set of rapids. Unfortunately, that scene was cut because it was a little too real. Fortunately, no one was hurt in the making of that scene, just maybe some feelings. On a daily basis I found myself smiling ear-to-ear and loving every minute of it. We continued on with the series and pushed into the jungle. On one particular day, the film crew was falling behind, we were soaked from rain and sweat and we were trying to get to our check point where we were going to set up camp for the night, when one of the guys started to get cold and I was worried about him getting hyperthermia (yep, you can even get hyperthermia in the jungle). I ran ahead with my pack, scouting it out, then ran back to pick up the stragglers with the extra gear. Once we finally got everyone into camp it was essentially dark. One of my scientists was shivering and getting goose bumps. My mind kicked into mission mode and right out of TV mode. We needed fire and shelter ASAP. I took out my hatchet and started to cut down thick vines to use as logs. They were basically the size of small logs that we could split up as firewood. I cut a few down and got a fire started. I directed guys to start clearing out the area and setting up their shelters. I continued to work on the fire, splitting the logs up. I was using my fixed blade knife to split the wood - a technique I had used for many years with no issues. It was raining and of course everything was wet. I attempted to set my knife into a log to split it just as I had done the 10 logs before, but my knife slipped and slid into the top of my hand like a hot knife through butter. At first I thought it wasn't that bad. The medic came over and we assessed the situation. Once we got the bleeding to stop and we could see inside I saw that my tendons had been severed, actually 3 tendons and a nerve. It was over just as fast as it had begun. I felt like I had found the meaning of life, seconds before I died. Here I was deep in the Amazon jungle, having the time of my life, finding my passion and it was suddenly over. I was devastated. I felt like I had let everyone down; my cast and crew, my team back home, and Miss Capra who really was the one that made this happen because she knew what I would find if I went.

At this point I had a choice. I could accept the defeat. I could accept where I was and the situation I was in and resign or I could use the information that I was now armed with. I had just found my passion. I decided that I was not about to leave that in the jungle like that. I still feel fortunate to have found the one thing that lights a fire in my belly somewhere as unlikely as Bolivia, doing a job I hadn't even initially bothered to apply for. So armed with this new knowledge about myself and my passion in life we completely changed the direction of my company. It was hard for people to understand the reasoning behind this decision because it was not the direction they had signed up for. We had hardly any equipment for this new media-oriented company and we hardly had a follower base outside the world of guns and tactical training. It was almost as if we were starting from scratch. The company as it stood was not progressing the way it should have been anyway. We were not growing a sustainable business model and something had to change. When I sat down with our staff to discuss the change it was not really well received, as I mentioned above. At the end of the day everyone left. We went from having a team of six people to being just Miss Capra and me. It was quite a blow, but change sometimes hurts and those that follow me on social media know that I say to embrace the change and embrace the pain that comes along with it. That is how we learn and that is how we grow. Growth hurts since we are stretching past our norms. Old things have to give way in order for growth to happen. Embrace it.

The opportunity to work with a film crew in Bolivia left me with four months of recovery and plenty of time to really think about what I wanted to do with my life as we started to produce. Miss Capra has a film degree from Full Sail and she also had a few pieces of gear that she didn't sell from her wedding videography business, which she left behind in Kansas City. We decided we just needed to start somewhere so I just filmed everything. I filmed my recovery, I filmed trips, I filmed anything that I could think. I was not even good at it and I wasn't using the stuff I filmed. I just knew this is what I wanted to do. Every day

I got a little better and every day another opportunity would come our way keeping us in business and moving us to the next month. This is until it got to a point where we went all in with production on my YouTube channel. We facilitated a plan to go all in and realized that if we did not make it in a year then we would basically be out of business. No pressure… However, when you are doing what you love and what you are passionate about it, it is hard to fail. Even failure doesn't feel like failure. It will feel more like learning what works and what doesn't. I look back now and see all the missteps and things that did not work and I still believe there was no way we were going to fail over-all because I was doing something that I truly loved. Even if doing this meant living in a van down by the river (I hope you know what that means).

My point with all of this is that you need to find that thing that makes you excited to get out of bed in the morning. That drives your heart to continue to move you forward. Maybe your passion might just start out by being a love of the journey through life and that is okay. Your mission might be to be patient as you work through different things that may or may not turn out to be your passion. It was not a direct road for me, but I found it and you know what? My passion might just change in 5 years and that is okay, too. As long as I'm focusing on what I love in life right now my life will be one worth living. Our existence on this earth is so short in the grand scheme of things. So why waste life on stressors that are really not even relevant to you?

MOVING FORWARD

If you get anything out of this book, I want it to be this: you are in control of your life. You are the captain of your ship and don't let anyone or anything dictate your direction. Anything worth having is worth working for. Nothing is owed to you, but you do deserve everything you work for. Sometimes that means having less or shedding some weight, so you can continue up the mountain. Maybe you do need to live in a van down by the river or sleep in the gym while you grow your business. Don't let fear dictate your happiness or direction.

You might still be in the middle of transitioning from one chapter of your life to another as you read this. I feel for you. I have been there. I know that it sucks and that you don't know if things will ever get better. But they will if you are willing to put in the hard work. You need to make it through the 7 stages and get to a point where you can start taking care of yourself again. Each step has its own challenges, but they all teach us something about ourselves and about life. It is 100% possible for you to find happiness and success even if you have been through some terrible, life-altering events. You have the ability to change the direction of your life at any point.

You just need to make that decision and put in the work.

Remember that we don't have to conquer everything in one day. We just need to make that one-inch step in a forward direction on a daily basis. We ultimately just need to find ourselves getting a better night's sleep. Eating healthier meals. Getting in shape for the life we want to live. Chasing our passion in life.

-Never Quitting

-Never Surrendering

-Always Moving Forward

ABOUT THE AUTHOR

Nick is a true renaissance man. Since his challenging youth experiences, through his time as a RECON and MARSOC Marine, and since his separation from the CORPs, he's been pushing the envelope of personal development. His unique perspective on life has enabled him to accomplish great things.

Nick now is an entrepreneur, philanthropist, producer, creator, and father of two beautiful women. He and his wife Miss Capra spend their time traveling the globe making videos and telling the stories of the present and past.

Connect with Nick Koumalatsos:

 nickkoumalatsos.com

 youtube.com/nickkoumalatsos

 facebook.com/nickkoumalatsos82

 instagram.com/nickkoumalatsos

 twitter.com/nickkoumalatsos

CPSIA information can be obtained
at www.ICGtesting.com
Printed in the USA
LVHW021919240619
622140LV00014B/474